Teaching Right from Wrong

40 Things You Can Do to Raise a Moral Child

ARTHUR DOBRIN

BERKLEY BOOKS, NEW YORK

Permission to reprint quoted selections were granted by the following:
Acts of Compassion by Robert Wuthnow copyright © 1991 by Princeton University Press.
Two stories adapted from *Love Your Neighbor: Stories of Value and Virtues* by Authur Dobrin. Reprinted by permission of Scholastic Inc.
Lest Innocent Blood Be Shed copyright © by Philip Hallie, HarperCollins Publishers Inc.
Golden Rules copyright © by Wayne Dosick, HarperCollins Publishers Inc.
The Prophet by Kahlil Gibran copyright © 1923 by Kahlil Gibran and renewed 1951 by Administrators CTA of Kahlil Gibran Estate and Mary G. Gibran. Reprinted by permission of Alfred A. Knopf, a Division of Random House Inc.
Descartes' Error: Emotion, Reason, and the Human Brain by Antonio Damasio, G.P. Putnam's Sons, 1994.
Moral Judgment of the Child by Jean Piaget, The Free Press, 1965.

A Berkley Book
Published by The Berkley Publishing Group
A division of Penguin Putnam Inc.
375 Hudson Street
New York, New York 10014

This book is an original publication of The Berkley Publishing Group.

Copyright © 2001 by Arthur Dobrin

PRINTING HISTORY
Berkley trade paperback edition / May 2001

The Penguin Putnam Inc. World Wide Web site address is
www.penguinputnam.com

Library of Congress Cataloging-in-Publication Data

Dobrin, Arthur, 1943–
    Teaching right from wrong : 40 things you can do to raise a moral child / Arthur Dobrin.
        p. cm.
    Includes bibliographical references and index.
    ISBN 0-425-17822-6
    1. Moral development. 2. Child rearing. I. Title

BF723.M54 D63 2001
649'.7—dc21   2001025102

PRINTED IN THE UNITED STATES OF AMERICA

10   9   8   7   6   5   4   3   2   1

To all the children I have loved

Contents

Preface

When Kenneth Starr's report on President Clinton was issued in September 1998, I received an invitation to appear on CNN to help parents talk to their children about the sex scandal. What do you say to your child about extramarital relations and about lying? And when two teenagers in Littleton, Colorado, murdered their own schoolmates, I was asked by several newspapers to comment on this. Are we raising a generation of monsters? What causes children to turn to murderous violence?

The answers aren't easy. For the real issues regarding morality go deeper than those prompted by the president's infidelity or whether we should have more control over guns. Morality is far more complex than equating it with sexual behavior or deadly weapons in the hands of children. And it certainly is far deeper than the legislation in Louisiana making youths address their elders as "Ma'am" and "Sir."

Ethics is about respect and courage, fairness and compassion. It is about principles and character, feelings, and reason. It is about individual responsibility and social justice. It is about how one leads one's life.

Clearly, though, when so many public figures bend the rules to suit their own needs and when children turn guns on their schoolmates, the concern for raising a moral child is more important than ever.

There are two basic elements in being a moral person: caring and making sound judgments. Caring develops out of the feelings and emotions we have as very young children. Here is love and compassion and being moved by the plight of other people. Caring is what we mean when we say a person has a good heart.

Sound judgment comes out of learning how to think clearly and independently. Moral judgment is a specific kind of intelligence and can be learned just as other forms of intelligence can be learned. Sound judgment is what we mean when we say someone is thoughtful. It is the ability to choose wisely between sometimes competing claims. While caring is like a good house foundation, sound judgments make up the building's frame.

When we take heart and mind together, when feelings and thoughts are blended in a person who both is responsive to the suffering of other individuals and takes their interests into account, acting benevolently and justly, we have a moral person.

The basic inspiration for this book comes from two studies from the Holocaust, *The Altruistic Personality,* by Samuel and Pearl Oliner, and *Conscience and Courage,* by Eva Fogelman. These works examine the backgrounds of people in Nazi Europe termed "rescuers." These were people, not Jewish themselves, who, at great risk, offered safe havens to Jews.

These two books come to several fundamental conclusions. One is that the perception of oneself as being able to do something about life's condition is a prerequisite for altruistic behavior. This, in turn, rests on relating to others in a supportive way. These conditions predispose a person to act ethically, because being part of a larger whole provides meaning and purpose to living. The rescuers also had one or more of the following characteristics: a nurturing, loving home in childhood; an altruistic parent or beloved caretaker; a tolerance for people who were different; a childhood illness or loss that tested their resilience; and an emphasis on independence, discipline with explanations, and caring.

The values they shared were altruism, independence of mind, and respect for differences among people. As children, the rescuers were taught these principles as part of daily living.

In *Teaching Right from Wrong* I have taken the implications from these and other studies from the field of moral psychology and have made them available to those interested in the practicalities.

One of the major conclusions reached by people who study the psychology of morality is that morality is acquired over time. It is similar to other developmental processes that children go through. Just as you can't expect a typical kindergartner to do algebra, you can't expect a five-year-old to know that breaking one cup out of spite is worse than breaking five cups accidentally. And just as you can't expect an elementary-school pupil to understand the theory behind arithmetic, you can't expect a ten-year-old to get to a deep understanding of ethics. Morality takes time to mature, and the direction and timing of maturity are generally predictable.

This book is a manual for raising an ethical child. It isn't a step-by-step parenting book, though. No book about people can be that, for every person is unique and every situation different. But there are generalities that apply and are more or less useful to everyone.

By using this book, not as a map but as a guide, I think that the person—whether parent, teacher, or anyone who comes into contact with children—who cares about raising ethical children can be helped in one of the most significant roles he or she can play.

Introduction

At the center of this book are the convictions that character can be shaped and stimulated by others and that parents, teachers, peers, and the larger culture in general all play an important part in molding and instilling moral values in children. At the same time, I believe that moral development is a natural process, as much a part of growing up as is learning a mother tongue. I say this despite the recent research on genetics and twins that suggests that far more is controlled by our genes than many have previously thought. In the age-old debate about nature and nurture, we are still largely in the dark regarding what we owe to our genes and what to our environment. This is just as true in the area of moral development as in any other area of human psychology, although most of us, parents and psychologists alike, continue to side with the nurturers. This is the reason why concerned parents are so eager to have their children attend good schools and are willing to pay high taxes or private-school tuition to see that they have a good education.

In recent years there has been a renewed push for character education. Many are upset by what they see in society, the daily news reports of scandal, deception, and violent crime. What is happening to society? Where are our moral standards? Are we raising a group of selfish, hedonistic, uncaring children who don't know the difference between right and wrong?

However much agreement there is about the fact that raising moral children is important, there is much disagreement about the solutions to the problem. Some criticize schools for not teaching values; some attack schools for teaching the wrong values. Some want schools to promote particular values; others believe that teaching values belongs in the home. Some blame TV, the Internet, and video games for the evils they see; others put all the blame on parents.

Is there such a thing as ethical education or is it a quixotic venture? It is hard enough to teach children reading and arithmetic, physics and biology, but at least in these subjects there is a general agreement about the desired outcomes. We know whether children have mastered the subject matter. Almost no one disagrees that SATs measure math skills more or less accurately. There is less agreement about shaping character or imparting values. Moral education isn't like the neat lawn of math but like a weedy field with bogs and stands of trees. Whose values are to be promoted, which characteristics are most desirable? Who is to teach it? Should education be for the benefit of the individual child or for society? Is religious instruction necessary for raising a moral person? And if so, whose religion is it that is to be promoted?

These are difficult and perplexing questions. But despite the apparent and substantive differences between liberals and conservatives, I think there is often more agreement about what constitutes a moral person and how to raise one than is commonly acknowledged. We can see this if we specify some of the characteristics of an ethical person. Good character is composed of the mix of the qualities of trustworthiness and kindness, responsibility and fairness. It may come in a sweet or rough package, but good character is a quality that ultimately allows one human being to count on another. There is also broad agreement that a loving child is most likely one who has been loved and a person who brutalizes others may well have been brutalized by others as a child. So although we may have little to say in whether our children prefer chocolate to vanilla, comedy to tragedy, and math to literature, we actually have much to say about whether our children will be moral in the broadest and deepest sense of the word.

It is also my conviction that the qualities I am talking about are universal. They aren't moral qualities admired by Europeans but not by Africans, for example. They aren't merely a reflection of my own biases. I can present my reasons for taking this position by referring to numerous studies in the field of moral psychology, and many of these will be found in the body of this book. But here I want instead to present my position more personally. My wife, Lyn, and I were in the Peace Corps in the 1960s and at that time worked with peasant farmers in western Kenya in East Africa. Through our work in adult education, we met Joshua and Raili Ongesa. I was attempting to form a cooperative for soapstone carvers in Joshua's village, and Lyn was teaching childcare and nutrition. After two years, my wife and I returned to the United States but stayed in touch with the Ongesas through letters; when we decided to return ten years later with our two children for a five-month stay, the Ongesas arranged for us to live down the road from them. When we arrived, we had no furniture, so they brought us one of their beds to use. The same with everything else. They had little, but what they had they willingly and unsparingly shared. They have never asked for anything in return. They are people with open hearts and a generous spirit. In all the years we have known each other, they have always been truthful. They are true to their word, thoroughly dependable, and above reproach. Of all the people I've known, they are among the kindest and most trustworthy.

For more than thirty years now we have maintained a relationship with the Ongesas, having returned to visit many times since. Joshua and Raili Ongesa speak no English, so we struggle with the Swahili that slips away from disuse or rely on one of their children to translate our English for them. Although they are monogamous, they come from families where polygamy is commonplace. One of Joshua's brothers has several wives, and while we were there we knew the senior chief, who had thirteen wives and more than fifty children. The Ongesas have twelve children and live in a house not much larger than my living room; we belong to different religions. The two of them have never been any further than Nairobi, 250 miles from their home near Lake Victoria. Joshua tends a meager plot of coffee trees, serves as his church's president, and makes some additional money by carving soapstone objects. Raili manages the family's financial resources by going to market to sell the maize, beans, and bananas she grows on their two-acre homestead.

Despite these and other differences in our cultures and life experiences, my family and theirs have become more than friends. We now think of ourselves as family. A grandchild of theirs was named Morris, after my late father-in-law, and I have a picture of their youngest son on the wall in my living room. What attracted me to the Ongesas? Why did we become so close and remain so all these years? It is their sweetness and sincerity, their open-heartedness and decency, the generosity of their spirit and their kindness. It is their steadfastness and dependability. I wish the world were filled with Ongesas.

I've sometimes wondered if I love them because they possess Western virtues. I don't think this is so. When I asked other people in the Kisii who they admired and trusted, the Ongesas topped most of the lists. Similarly, many of the people I didn't like or trust in Kenya were the same ones that others spoke about derisively. What seems true to me is that a good person is a good person and a scoundrel a scoundrel wherever you go. To be sure there are cultural differences—eating with the fingers or with forks, initiating into adulthood by circumcision or by getting a driver's license, eating termites or lobsters. But I think these are the differences that make life interesting. Underneath this resides the bedrock of character, and this I think is similar throughout the world. People everywhere face the same problems in life: eating properly, fending off illness, and getting along with others. When we work well together, humanity prospers. Those who promote this through their actions of beneficence, caring, sharing, and justice are the people we most admire.

My own thinking about morality roughly follows the approach of one of the leading researchers in the field of moral development, James Rest of the Center for the Study of Ethical Development at the University of Minnesota. There are four major determinants of moral behavior, Rest states. First is the awareness that our actions affect other people. Second is the ability to make judgments between possible courses of action. Third is being sufficiently motivated to want to do the right thing. And fourth is having the ego, strength, courage, and perseverance to follow through on wanting to act ethically. For the sake of clarity, we can look at each of these streams by itself. In real life, however, they are not so much separate streams as separate currents in the same body of water. Together they constitute what we call *moral character*.

Parents play a substantial part in their children's moral development. As with many other aspects of raising children, we can use some guidance. Some things about raising moral children are obvious, but others aren't. While there is no prescription, no formula, and certainly no guarantee, I believe that there is an approach to ethical education that people can follow to help their children acquire the motivation, habits, judgment, and ability to be moral.

Parents, however, don't live in isolation. There is a larger social environment that also affects the moral development of children. So, although parents have a large impact on a child's moral development, they do so within a wider framework that either makes the task easier or more difficult. In a helpful society, parents find support for ethical values in schools, neighborhood, work, and cultural institutions. There are times, however, when for families the work of raising moral children is difficult. For example, raising a moral child is easier in a safe school than one where students are checked for guns. Because children also learn by imitation, it is difficult to have moral children when movies and TV are saturated with plots of greed than with ones of heroism.

It is my hope that this book will help those concerned with the moral development of children to better understand the components of ethical growth. I believe that this book will make clear that good behavior and being a moral person aren't always the same thing. What most people mean by "good behavior," especially as it applies to children, is that the person follows the family's or society's rules. So what being a good child often means is that the child does what he or she is told. "He's such a good boy," often means that Roger listens to what we say and obeys our commands. And a convicted criminal who is given probation for good behavior is a prisoner who cooperated with the authorities. In other words, "good" behavior frequently means "conforming" behavior.

"Ethical" behavior, in contrast, may or may not conform to the rules of society, as was clear with the rescuers of Jews. A whistle-blower is not a good employee, because she is risking the company's financial well-being, but she may well be a moral person. Good behavior is ethical behavior only when the rules being followed are themselves moral. The distinction is an important one, for adults sometimes confuse wanting a child to behave well with raising a moral child. This book will help parents and others concerned with children to better understand how to raise a child who they can be proud of, one who is not a bystander but a person whom others can admire for his moral character.

Feelings

Emotions Are the Groundwork
of Morality

Kindness is the courage to care.
—AUNG SAN SUU KYI, in *The Voice of Hope*

Before Jennifer can think, she feels. Before Kevin has thoughts, he has emotions. Before there are reasons, there are reactions. Feelings come first. Without them we cannot be ethical people. They are the seeds of moral development.

We must be touched by the lives of others to act morally. I'm not talking about liking other people. We may like someone or not. But we can still be moved by their fate and feel for their condition. We must be touched by them in some way—moved to a concern about their welfare—before we take the step of acting fairly or on their behalf. Without this connection, all else is beside the point.

There are various terms for this capacity to connect with others, but broadly I am talking about sympathy and empathy.

People who lack empathy, who cannot feel what another person feels, are cold and alienated. And cold, distant people disturb us because we are afraid they will let us down, turn away from us when we most need them, or break our hearts without even knowing or caring that they have. If morality means anything at all, it means being able to count on another person. As psychiatrist Willard Gaylin explains: "Feeling is—if not all—almost all. It serves utility and sensuality. Feelings are the fine instruments which shape decision-making in an animal cursed and blessed with intelligence, and the freedom which is its corollary. They are signals directing us toward goodness, safety, pleasure and group survival."

This is the ancient idea of the humanities, and I share the view of those who believe that feelings are the gatekeepers to the moral world. The philosopher Emmanuel Levinas believed that moral sensitivity comes before knowledge. Unlike the Cartesian formula, which stated "I think, therefore I am," Levinas wrote, "I am because I am in relation to others. The self is possible only in recognition of the Other." The implication is that our very existence depends on others. There is no self without an other.

Because humans can't survive alone, sensitivity toward the lives of other people may be innate. At least there are some biologists who think so. They claim that human beings have an instinctive affinity for other lives, even for lives that aren't human. Biologist E. O. Wilson coined the term *biophilia* to explain this phenomenon of feeling drawn toward other humans and creatures. You can see it as you watch an infant reacting to other babies and small animals. Watch people coo over cuddly animals. "Oh, how cute," we say about kittens and pups, baby gorillas and baby chimps. Our eyes well at the sight of harp seals being slaughtered because their eyes look so doleful, so human. And we break into smiles at the sight of human infants. I seldom hear anyone say that an infant is ugly. This isn't merely sparing the feelings of the parent. Infants are adorable simply because they are infants. We want to hold them and take care of them. Philosopher George Santayana said, "Nature kindly warps our judgment about our children, especially when they are young, when it would be a fatal thing if we did not love them."

These feelings may exist, the biologists say, because they provide a Darwinian advantage to the human species. They propel us to take care of infants who would die without help. Similar feelings of solidarity move us to bond to others. We willingly become parts of groups, because it is only through the cooperative efforts of people—people acting in concert—that humans are able to compete successfully in an environment in which, prehistorically, other creatures are bigger and stronger. Even today, no person can survive alone. Even Robinson Crusoe needed his Man Friday and the most self-reliant person is piggybacking on the advances made by others. Cooperative and self-abnegating behavior allows humans to act more efficiently, because it is only in concert that humans are able to get what they need. Of course, humans are also competitive and aggressive. But the instinct that bonds us to others must also be present. Human biology, in other words, favors cooperation and self-sacrifice. Altruism is built into our genes. We are born with the capacity to identify with others and the desire to be part of a group. This, in turn, requires a readiness to take in the rules and values of the group into which we are born. Here is the genesis of ethics. As explained by Frans de Waal, a primatologist,

> *We are born to absorb rules and values, many of which place community interests above private ones. We have been selected for such profound internalization that these rules and values become literally our own. We have built-in mechanisms that frustrate attempts to cheat. No doubt these capacities evolved because they served a purpose in the highly cooperative and trust-based societies of our ancestors.*

If honesty didn't have a biologic edge over cheating, there couldn't be a successful society. In other words, we are emotionally and psychologically predisposed to be part of a group. It is this capacity to be open and responsive emotionally that we call empathy. It is a capacity that is present before we can reflect and judge. It is as close to instinct as humans get. Before the development of higher forms of thinking—the stages at which we can think abstractly and theoretically based on prior experience—there are feelings. They are immediate. Children don't think about how they will react to others. Something touches them and they respond. This is part of the charm of young children. It is why we think of them as innocent. They are guileless, nearly pure emotion. Young children may not be able to tell you what they think, but they certainly can't hide what they are feeling. It is all aboveboard. There is no guessing about their likes and dislikes, their pleasures and displeasure. "Strawberry, how icky!"

Our capacity to experience the world subjectively comes before our ability to think about what we experience.

Ethics of the heart may well first show itself even in the youngest of children. If you have ever seen a group of infants or watched young children in a nursery, you may have noticed what psychologists call "global empathy," a term coined by Martin Hoffman. There is a kind of contagion of distress that works its way through the nursery room. The cries of one newborn will often set off cries in other infants. The first child is experiencing something upsetting (hunger or pain of some kind) and the other newborns seem to be affected by the sounds of distress. Others begin to cry, as though the disquietude they hear were upsetting to them. This may be nothing more than agitation, or it may be a precursor to empathy. Hoffman thinks the response does lead to genuine empathy because many toddlers, when hearing or seeing others in distress, actually offer gestures intended to provide comfort. Why does this happen? No one knows for certain. But it may be a primitive and instinctive kind of emotional sharing.

Interestingly, not all infants respond this way. And no one knows if children who do seem to resonate with the distress of others turn out to be more caring as adults. But whether at this point or at another, the ability to feel hurt whenever another is hurting—to empathize and genuinely sympathize—is the very foundation of morality itself. The ability to be distressed by another's pain is one of the strong motives that leads people to help those who need our assistance, whether this is the accident victim, orphaned child or the frail elderly. George Eliot summed it nicely when she asked, "What is life for if not to make things easier for others?"

Every parent and teacher of young children knows that children are full of impulses and aggression. Adults are constantly intervening to put a stop to hitting, biting, and taking. Although young children are self-absorbed and egotistical, concentrated as they are on their own wants and pleasures, that isn't all there is to them. The emotional lives of young children are in fact quite complex. While a child believes that he is the center of the universe, that he lives in a place where his wishes should come first and foremost, there is another stream flowing through him that is just as natural as egotism. Samantha may want all the toys for herself, but at the same time she may also feel some sympathy for the child playing next to her. The child is both egotistical and altruistic at the same time.

Global empathy is amorphous, hesitant, and tentative. It is a kind of proto-feeling, an immature and unripened feeling that paves the way for other emotions. You could say that global empathy is to a full emotional life what crawling is to walking. And just as crawling gives way to walking, global empathy is supplanted sometime during a child's second year by tenderness and other gentle feelings.

This proto-feeling of global empathy grows into something larger around age two. Kevin will make approaches to others who are in distress. He will turn toward cries, make tentative approaches, and appear to feel distress himself. Some children even go as far as attempting to comfort the person who is upset. Siblings will sometimes try to make their upset brothers or sisters laugh, presumably as a means of making them feel better. Empathy seems to be largely involuntary, is rewarding for its own sake, and operates outside of cognitive processing. In other words, sympathy bubbles up from within all by itself.

An extensive study at the National Institute of Mental Health found that during the second year children become increasingly sensitive to the distress of family members. The older children in the study were more likely to do something about someone else's pain. After eighteen months, toddlers responded with prosocial behavior about one third of the time. By the time children are two, they are responsive about half the time.

At this age, differences between boys and girls become increasingly apparent. They tend to play with different toys and express different interests. Are they also different in regard to empathy? Many parents think so, and they may be right. It was certainly true of my own children. I remember when my daughter, Kori, was about three and son, Eric, was five. My wife had banged her head and was sitting on the floor in pain. Kori came over and tried to comfort her. Eric walked over to her and asked her to help him with something. But no one knows for sure whether there really is a difference between the sexes. Sometimes conventional wisdom is questioned when it is examined a little more closely. In one study, for example, young girls did score higher than boys in terms of empathy; but in another, researchers found that in daycare settings, boys were more responsive to another's distress than girls. So it may turn out that the differences we see between males and females depend on the settings. It is useful to keep this in mind so we don't fall into the trap of saying, "Oh, boys will be boys." Stereotypes aren't helpful here. If compassion is the groundwork of ethical behavior, as I think it is, then we can't let boys off the hook with a reference to their supposed nature. We don't know what the nature of boys and girls is in regard to morality.

As you can see, empathy evolves over time. The next step along the way starts at age two or three. Now Jennifer and Kevin begin to understand that they and the physical and social world are not the same. For the first time, they realize that others have feelings and thoughts of their own. Yet until somewhere between six and nine years old, their sympathetic responses are still specific to particular situations. If their feelings have been properly educated, if someone on the street is hurt, they'll stop to help. But if you try to get them to understand that there are other people who also need their assistance but who aren't right in front of them, you will probably draw a blank stare. They simply can't imagine that. If they see a homeless person, they may want to give him money. But your talk about hungry people in other parts of the world will fall on deaf ears. It is only when Jennifer and Kevin reach adolescence that they can broaden their concern to encompass humanity. Only then can they be moved by people whom they have not met or who are not part of their group.

The question still remains: Does sympathy in fact lead to ethical behavior? Common sense tells us that there is a connection and the little research on the question does point in a direction that supports our hunch. The Oliner study, mentioned in the "Preface," found that about one third of the people they interviewed said they became rescuers because sympathy, compassion, and pity moved them. The Oliners found that rescuers did not think they were more socially responsible than bystanders. Where rescuers differed significantly from nonrescuers, however, was the extent to which they identified with others' pain. Rescuers were tuned in to the emotional states of other people more keenly than were nonrescuers.

What I have been presenting here is the idea that whatever list of virtues we may ultimately accept as most important, all morality must have at a minimum a component of caring. To care is to be related in an emotional way and without that emotional connection, acting morally becomes a dubious undertaking. Emmanuel Kant went so far as to write that if a person were completely lacking in moral feeling "he would be morally dead. And if . . . the life-force could no longer excite this feeling, then humanity would dissolve."

What is it like to be morally dead? Antonio Damasio's fascinating clinical examples from his work as a neurologist at the

University of Iowa College of Medicine address this point. In one unsettling account, he relates the story of Elliot, a man in his thirties whom Damasio was asked to see after the man experienced a change of personality after brain surgery. Elliot had been a successful professional who had served as a role model for younger colleagues and had been happily married and a good father. Surgery removed a tumor the size of an orange from his prefrontal lobe. However, like the bad joke about hospital care, the operation was a success but the patient died. Not that Elliot literally died; the biologic entity was saved but somehow Elliot just wasn't Elliot any longer. His mental faculties were intact, but his personality had been so altered that his life was now in disarray. By the time Damasio saw him, Elliot had been divorced and remarried several times, was living with a sibling, and was incapable of holding a job.

Elliot needed pushing to rouse himself from bed in the morning; he couldn't keep to a schedule at work. His work was constantly behind schedule because some detail captured his attention. He would lose track of the main point of his activity, getting so caught up in side issues that he seldom finished his job. He then went into business for himself, but he encountered one set-back after another. He went bankrupt ignoring warnings from his friends that his ventures were imprudent. Despite his intelligence and knowledge, Elliot was now acting the fool. He had business knowledge but no longer had business sense. His judgment was impaired. More important, he lacked the will to do anything about it. It was as though he were shrugging his shoulders, saying, "Who cares? It makes no difference to me what happens."

What was going on? His memory was fully intact. Was Elliot lazy, depressed, or feeling sorry for himself?

Damasio suspected that Elliot's change in behavior was not rooted in some flaw in his character, but rather was a result of the surgery itself. Something had been damaged in Elliot's brain. Damasio conducted a battery of standard tests to measure intelligence. Elliot performed normally or above on all of them. He was also given standard tests to measure his personality. He proved normal on those, too, Damasio then turned his attention from Elliot's intelligence to his emotions.

> *Elliot was able to recount the tragedy of his life with a detachment that was out of step with the magnitude of the events. He was always controlled, always describing scenes as a dispassionate, uninvolved spectator. Nowhere was there a sense of his own suffering, even though he was the protagonist. . . . In some curious, unwitting protective way, he was not pained by his tragedy. Elliot was far more mellow in his emotional display now than he had been before his illness. He seemed to approach life on the same neutral note. . . . He told me without equivocation that his own feelings had changed from before his illness. He could sense how topics that once had evoked a strong emotion no longer caused any reaction, positive or negative. . . . We might summarize Elliot's predicament as to know but not to feel. . . . I began to believe that the cold-bloodedness of Elliot's reasoning prevented him from assigning different values to different options, and made his decision-making landscape hopelessly flat.*

In his book *Descartes' Error*, Damasio spells out the connection between emotion and the neural system and its various components. It is his firm conviction that emotions play a basic role in rational behavior. Without emotions we would be like Elliot: possessing the intelligence to analyze but lacking the emotional depth to be interested enough to put the skill to good use. Everything would be equal; nothing would be more valuable or important than anything else. We simply wouldn't care. We would know we are making a mess of our marriages, and we wouldn't be motivated to do anything about it. Our social lives would be in shambles, we would understand what we had done to make it so, but we would continue letting others down because we lacked the will to keep our good character intact.

Fortunately, few of us are Elliots. If we are neurally intact, we possess emotions and feelings, which help us adapt successfully to social situations. We can choose one thing or the other because one thing matters to us more than another does. Feelings allow us to possess a value system, to prize one thing over another, to have a set of moral priorities. What Elliot's tragedy demonstrates is that the ability to feel is more than a condition for prosocial behavior. It is a prerequisite.

When we feel for someone, when we are touched, we want to act on his behalf. But the capacity to feel—to care—also is more than a motivation for action. For it is possible for someone to go through the motions and do the right thing but still get it wrong, so to speak. This is the distinction between the letter of the law and its spirit. Although doing the right thing is vital, it is also important that it be done with the correct feeling. There are exceptions, of course, such as a gifted surgeon who may care about nothing but her reputation and fee. In some cases, competency outweighs kindness. More typically, though, most of us want to be treated by doctors as though our feelings counted. Most of us want a physician who not only is a skilled practitioner but also takes the time to show us that she cares about us as individuals. This demonstration of caring is the quality that makes you want to confide in your doctor. You feel that you will be responded to as a full human being.

A negligent spouse, a wastrel, or drunkard has failed his duty as a husband. But something is also absent from the dutiful wife who does what she does only because it is expected of her. Children long to be held, to be kissed on the brow, to feel a gentle hand on the shoulder. In significant relationships, we want people to act from the heart as well as acting wisely. If we don't believe in the sincerity of the person offering us help, we tend to reject the offer. It feels as though we were being pitied or patronized. It is the feeling tone of a relationship that is a piece of what makes the relationship a moral one.

Professor of philosophy at Georgetown University Nancy Sherman writes, "The point of helping in many . . . cases is to reassure another that we care—to show patience, loyalty, considerateness, empathy. Here the quality of the emotional interaction is inseparable from the act of helping." To paraphrase Robert Frost, the world may die of fire but our souls may die first of ice.

It seems clear to me that emotions are essential for ethics. This raises a question, though. Is there any way to educate the heart? I believe that feelings, like so many other attributes that make us human, can be either nourished or stifled. Most of us know this when we think of the negative examples. A child who is yelled at frequently learns quite well what anger is. And a child who is ignored often learns coldness. It doesn't take much persuading to convince us that we can easily cause children to shut off their feelings, close off the world, and become insensitive to others. Our early feelings of empathy leave us vulnerable. Too frequent harsh words, cross looks, and arbitrary punishment can twist incipient feelings of care into harsh feelings of cynicism and cruelty. One psychologist contends that children from homes where expressiveness is punished learn how to suppress their feelings and feel anxious in emotionally charged situations. The child's innate sensitivity is being channeled not into empathy but into personal distress. This is a child who may be full of feelings but lacks empathy, as she has no way of understanding what she is feeling. Emotions can turn to empathy when they are given proper social meaning.

There are many things that you can do to take advantage of your child's natural inclination toward sympathy and empathy.

1.

Tune In to Your Children's Feelings

From the time Kevin and Jennifer are born, they have feelings. So you can't begin moral education too soon. Feelings, remember, are the foundation of an ethical life.

Feelings come before speech; they come before reason. Children have feelings before they can express themselves verbally, long before they can form concepts.

Feelings can be cultivated into empathy, the ability to imagine what it is like to walk in another's shoes. When you tune in to your child's feelings, you are serving as a terrific role model of what it means to be empathetic. You are helping your child along the road to moral behavior. This is the very basis of ethics.

Because feelings arise before the ability to think about them, it is important for you as a parent to acknowledge the feelings your child has, then comment on them and label them. Children don't *understand* their feelings, although they have them. By helping children to identify their feelings, they can begin to understand that others have the same feelings as they do.

One day, not-yet-three-year-old Jennifer was with her grandmother. "Oh, no, just look at that!" her grandmother said as she saw someone throw trash from a car.

"You're angry, Grandma," Jennifer said.

Her grandmother didn't say she was angry. Yet Jennifer was able to correctly identify the emotion. She was able to put herself in her grandmother's place because Jennifer's mother had made it a practice to identify her own and Jennifer's emotions. Jennifer was on her way to real empathy.

Religious leaders tell us to love our neighbor as ourself. This is based on the idea that other people have feelings, wants, and desires just as we do. If you are unaware of your own feelings, there isn't much of a chance that you will know what others desire, want, and need.

It is easy to overlook the importance of feelings in children. Feelings sometimes frighten us. So when our children are overwhelmed by strong feelings, especially negative ones, we want to dampen them down, hoping to get control. "I hate Kevin!" Jennifer shouts, and we might be tempted to say something like, "No, you don't hate Kevin. Kevin is your brother." But this really isn't helpful. At the moment Jennifer blurts this out, she does hate Kevin. To tell her that she isn't experiencing that feeling is to make her doubt the validity of her own feelings. And if she isn't sure what she is feeling herself, there isn't much chance that she'll be able to correctly identify what others are feeling.

It is best to acknowledge that Jennifer does hate Kevin at that moment. State what you see going on, then talk about what has made her feel this way and what can be done about it.

If the feelings are suppressed and pushed out of sight, they get buried in the unconscious and come out later in ways that we don't understand and can do little to control. Negative feelings can be demons but we are best able to deal with them when we can see them and understand them.

So instead of saying, "No, you don't hate Kevin," it is better to say, "You are really angry at Kevin right now." This acknowledges the feelings that Jennifer really has. You want to legitimize her having feelings and you want her to correctly identify those feelings. At the same time, you want Jennifer to learn that the feeling, no matter how negative or hostile, can be turned into something positive if it is properly directed. So you want to talk to her about what made her angry and what can be done to alter the situation so the feeling will change. Everything else being equal, even young children recognize that it feels better to be happy than it does to be angry and so will be grateful with the help you give them in changing the feeling from a negative to a positive one.

2.

- - - - - - - - -

Talk About How You Think Others
May Be Feeling

Feelings are critical to us because, as some biologists point out, they provide survival skills to the human species. Feelings move us to bond to others, and it is only in groups that humans can survive.

Altruism—helping others willingly, without expectation of reward—is built into our genes. It comes first from our feelings, as we extend outward to become part of a group.

The capacity to be open and responsive emotionally is present before our ability to reflect and judge. Before the development of higher forms of thinking—the stages at which we can think abstractly and theoretically based on prior experience—there are feelings.

Talking about what others are feeling helps keep before a child the unspoken world and brings the unconscious to light. The talking keeps feelings from slipping into total invisibility later in life. It is when feelings are hidden and out of view that they are most dangerous.

When Jennifer takes away Kevin's toy, she may not know for sure what Kevin is feeling. So we may say something like, "I don't think Kevin likes what you've done. He doesn't look very happy to me. How do you think he feels?"

This helps Jennifer fine-tune an ability that she probably already possesses. Being attuned to others' feelings is natural for most people. It's almost as though feelings picked up vibrations transmitted by others transmit; as if we each had a built-in device for picking up those emissions. I believe that we are born with feeling receptors that operate even before our eyes do and the ability to feel is as important as our sight.

As with many other capacities, you as a parent can help strengthen it or allow it to wither. With proper attention to feelings, the ability to identify with others becomes deeper over time. Jennifer and Kevin will be able to imagine what it is like to stand in someone else's shoes.

3.

- - - - - - - - -

Comment on Your Own Emotions

Commenting on your own emotions helps your child think about his feelings, sort through them, and give them meaning. Letting your child know what you are feeling, why and what it means, is a large part of the moral education of a young child.

Infants have feelings but the feelings have no meaning in and of themselves. They are much like their responses to pleasure and pain—they are immediate, private, and direct. Little by little the chaos of unnamed feelings can be turned into a mature emotional life as you help your child become aware of the feelings you have.

Communication is more than talking about facts or ideas. Facts and ideas are important but, really, they are a small part of our lives. Most of what we do involves other people. We are constantly reacting to people on an emotional level—we like them, we don't like them, we care for them, we feel rejected by them.

Emotions continue to underlie a large part of our lives from infancy through old age. The question is whether we know what those emotions are and whether they lead us to better lives or remain below the surface and tie us in knots. We need to talk about feelings so we can turn them into productive emotions.

In general, girls have an easier time with their emotions than boys. The emotional lives of boys are too often given short shrift. The idea that men are more "rational" and women are more "emotional" is so deeply embedded in us that boys and girls express themselves differently from a very early age. Boys play with toy objects while girls play with toy children.

Because caring is the very foundation of morality, we can't

neglect the emotional lives of boys. We have to pay as much attention to the inner lives of our sons as we do to those of our daughters. This doesn't mean that boys should be given dolls instead of trucks, although there is no good reason why they shouldn't. But it does mean commenting on the feelings present in the family, talking about those feelings, making feelings legitimate, and learning how to express them, whether our children be boys or girls. "My boss was unhappy with my work today," we might say. "I'm feeling really sad."

Let me be clear here: I am not suggesting that it is important for every child to effusively express her feelings. Whether an angry Jennifer screams out what she is feeling or talks about it quietly is a matter of temperament and circumstance. Also, there are times when it is better not to vent one's feelings.

I'm talking about being aware of one's own and others' feelings. Some people are expressive, some reserved, some emotional, some intellectual. No one personality type is more inclined to be caring, considerate, or responsible. It is the *awareness* of feelings, not their expression, which makes the difference. "I'm glad that you're feeling happy today, Kevin," we can say, acknowledging his mood.

Talk to your child about what you and he are feeling. But never force your child to *express* his feelings, which may be contrary to his nature and, therefore, disrespectful of him. Feelings don't need to be laid out and displayed to be understood. Recognition and acknowledgment of feelings can also be unstated and subtle.

4.

- - - - - - - -

Sing to and Hold Your Children

The earliest sound we hear, even before we are born, is the sounds of our mother's heartbeat. Soon after birth, the rhythm is given form in melody. These are the lullabies that babies hear—the human voice expressing protection and devotion. This is the same in the Kalahari Desert as it is in Chicago. Everywhere lullabies fill the night air, as mother and child touch, gazing into one another's eyes.

Just as infants are soothed by their mothers' heartbeats, babies are reassured by the songs they hear. There is rocking and touching, there is melody and words. All this is the reassurance that makes love possible.

Close contact between adult and child is an essential part of healthy development. We know what happens to children who are kept at a distance, without skin-to-skin contact. To be touched (literally) prepares the way for being touched (figuratively) by the situations of other people.

Songs have ways of staying with us, outlasting most everything else. They arrive unbidden in the strangest places; we find ourselves singing songs we thought we'd long forgotten; we sing songs that remind us of people and places. We sing songs that fill our hearts with love and longing.

The road from song to morality is through love and happiness. If Kevin is a happy, loved child, he will more quickly respond to the needs of others than if he harbors hurts and nurses rejections. Because someone who is loved and happy will more naturally feel expansive and be less suspicious of others than the disgruntled person and, therefore, is more likely to respond when others need him.

The great American psychologist and philosopher William James once wrote, "I don't sing because I'm happy; I'm happy because I sing." James is right. Singing even when not happy makes us happy, because it is a kind of self-fulfilling prophecy. The very act of singing brings on the condition we desire. So even if you are feeling down, sing. It deepens and lifts the spirits.

"A song will outlive all sermons in the memory," a clergyman once observed. This is true not only about religion but about our personal lives as well. Everyone can sing songs from her childhood but barely remember a lecture. Music and poetry together are able to pierce us the way nothing else can, and that piercing makes us more sensitive to the world around us. Songs reside close to the heart.

One of the first times my wife watched our granddaughter for the night, MacKenzie was inconsolable. Lyn paced the room with her but our granddaughter seemed beyond comforting . . . until Lyn began to sing to her. MacKenzie immediately fell quiet and was soon asleep. Now the nighttime ritual ends with two songs, the last one always the same, a mournful Yiddish melody about a bird searching for freedom.

So sing to your children. It is the road to understanding the language of the heart.

5.

Read Imaginative Stories to Your Children

Reading to children is good for their imagination, and an active imagination helps develop empathy. Empathy is, after all, being able to *imagine* what it is like to be another person. To empathize with another requires a leap from your own experience into that of another. This is exactly what good stories do—bring us sympathetically into the lives of other, different lives.

Imaginative literature—stories with strong characters—is a particularly rich source for cultivating empathy. As novelist Julia Alvarez writes, fiction is "but a way to travel through the human heart."

Young children who are read to are set on a road to deepened feelings. Television also tells stories, but by its very nature, it is passive and impersonal. TV doesn't talk to you and doesn't care about you. But to hear stories and to feel the presence of an adult at the same time is to be doubly touched—first by the story and second by the storyteller.

My family had few books in the home, yet some of my fondest memories revolve around reading and being read to. I remember my mother sitting beside me when I was sick with fever and reading a story to me as I drowsed. I don't recall what she read but I was comforted by her presence and by the sound of her voice. I could escape my own unhappiness by entering into another life and do it with my mother at my side. By being read to, we are able to enter into an unfamiliar world, yet feel secure in doing it because a trusted adult is at our side.

Later, when I had children of my own, I told them tales and read to them as a way of sending them off to what I hoped would be pleasant dreams and memories as deeply embedded as mine. In their own minds, they could now be in a far-off place and feel what that was like; they would hear about hippos who were friends and listen to stories about living in hotels.

Children who never read about little engines that could or wild things or frogs who care about each other or rabbits at tea parties are missing something more than pleasure. They are deprived of part of their moral education.

Moral stories don't have to be stories with a moral. A story doesn't have to have a moral to it to make it good for ethical education. Writer John Bayley explains why. "What I understand by an author's love for his characters is a delight in their independent existence as *other people,* an attitude towards them which is analogous to our feelings towards those we love in life; an intense interest in their personalities combined with a sort of detached solicitude, a respect for their freedom."

Our lives can be changed by fiction, our character molded because we cared about one other person, even if that person is unlikable. Caring about fictional characters prepares us to care about real people. When we are immersed in a book, the characters are alive for us. We cry or weep or become angry at their fate. Much the same could be said about other art forms, but I suspect that especially for children nothing quite matches engaging stories in their ability to forge the language of feelings, to touch the heart with tenderness.

Lucky are the children who have stories read to them, who are given fables and short stories and novels and books of poetry, who vicariously enter the lives of other people who are born and die in other times, in distant places or in neighborhoods just like their own. Lucky are they whose hearts are broken when Bambi's mother is shot by the hunter or follow the adventures of two boys on the Mississippi River or that of a yellow dog. These children don't know that they are learning moral lessons but they are. Reading a story for its own sake, they are absorbing deeper messages.

Literature is important in still another way. When a child

reads a book on her own, she takes it at her own pace, in her own space. This provides room for reflection, an opportunity to think unhurriedly, without pressure, a chance to think independent thoughts, to explore alternative ways of understanding and relating. While building an emotional groundwork, literature also helps establish a pattern of critical, reflective, and empathic thinking.

Go to your library. See what books it has for children. Take a look at the ones that have won awards, talk to the librarian, read reviews in magazines. Most bookstores have sections devoted to children's books. Spend time to see what is available. There is a wealth of terrific children's books these days. Bring some home; give them as gifts, read together, encourage your child to read alone.

Read a bedtime story. Make one up or let your children pick their own. Falling asleep to a parent's voice is one of the most pleasant ways for a young child to end the day.

Reason

Feelings Need to Be Guided by Reason

> The golden rule is to test everything in the light of reason and experience, no matter from whom it comes.
> —MOHANDAS GANDHI, *The International Dictionary of Thoughts*

Just as feelings lay the groundwork for caring, reason provides the groundwork for thoughtfulness.

I lived in Kenya in 1965, soon after its independence. In my small town, there was an Englishwoman who was packing her bags to return home after years of living in colonial privilege. She couldn't take her pedigree Airedale home with her and asked me and my wife if we would like Gypsy. She laid down one condition for our accepting the dog: If she had pups, we couldn't give them away but must sell them. This wasn't to make a profit, she said, but was a way of ensuring that those who took the puppies would be able to take care of them. This seemed reasonable to us and we readily made the promise. During the next year, we became close friends with a couple. Indeed, when our son was born, Armand became his godfather. Then Gypsy had her first litter and Armand asked for one of the whelps. We were happy that he wanted one but, keeping the promise we had made, we asked for a nominal amount. Armand didn't say anything to us, but our relationship deteriorated. We had no idea what had happened.

We returned to the United States and learned that Armand had moved to England. Many years later, my wife and I found Armand again, nearly by accident; only then did we discover the cause for the rupture. He had been deeply disappointed in us and extremely hurt by our request. If we were like brothers, how could I even think of charging him for the dog? For my part, I had made a promise; and by asking for a small sum, I thought I had arrived at a satisfactory compromise. I was giving Armand what he wanted and keeping the promise, all at the same time. Fortunately, we were then able to talk about the incident and to repair the damage my wife and I had thoughtlessly caused. I relate this anecdote because it is a tale of misunderstanding. This is about a conflict between a principle (keeping a promise, even if foolishly given) and a relationship.

Armand was operating from his heart; I was acting from my head. Generally, our feelings and our thoughts comingle and inform each other. Seldom do we find a person who is pure feeling or pure thought. Even those who are near one end of the spectrum still find their thoughts and feelings entangled. In fact, the interaction between them is so intimate that it is nearly impossible to know one without the other. What we know occurs in the setting of our emotions, and our emotions are informed by what we know. Nevertheless, we can look at them separately and in that way better understand both.

The reason we need reason is because there are times choices have to be made between conflicting feelings. Say Jennifer has been provoked by another child to the point at which she is bubbling with anger. But striking out, as she wants to do, isn't the way for her to settle the problem. The sorting out between one feeling and another—deciding that this is better than that— is a matter of judgment. And good judgment requires sound reason.

Emotions are the raw material of morality, but it takes reason to turn those feelings into ideas worthy of action.

So how does a child learn to distinguish between feelings,

which are appropriate to act on and which aren't? There are a variety of sources. Children learn from other children, and they learn from school. They learn from the primary adults in their lives, parents mainly; and they learn from television, music, and movies.

No child is born knowing the moral rules that govern society. Children need to learn what is acceptable and what is not. These cultural and safety rules are learned because someone has said, "No, you can't do that."

"But *why* can't I," Jennifer replies.

Psychologists Joan Grusec and Jacqueline Goodnow reviewed hundreds of studies that looked at the various ways parents discipline their children. What they found, with overwhelming consistency, was that successful parents placed substantial emphasis on reasoning. Their conclusions echo those of the Oliners and of Fogelman, who found that one of the things that distinguished the Holocaust rescuers from the bystanders is that their parents consistently offered explanations to go along with the discipline.

The opposite side of this coin is that parents who discipline their children with threats of force, intimidation, humiliation, or violence frequently fail in their goal of having loving, compassionate, caring, or even well-behaved children.

Children can't understand all the explanations that you give them. But they will become increasingly sophisticated in grasping your point. Just as I believe that there is universality to moral feelings, I believe that our brains function in such a way that there is progressive development to thinking, which unfolds with time. If you are patient and persistent in giving reasons, by the time your children are adolescents, they will understand most of what you mean. It is my belief that children come to moral judgments as naturally as they develop the ability to speak. The Swiss psychologist Jean Piaget first explored this idea. He found that a child's understanding of morality changes as the child matures.

You can use language as an analogy to understand Piaget's concept. An infant's first vocalizations are gurgles and noises. Then come goo-goo's and da-da's and these give way to simple sentences. Over time, children can express most of their desires and ideas and, later still, acquire language skills that straighten out syntax and grammar. Moral reasoning is much like that, Piaget found. At around five years old, children are concrete and simple, saying things such as, "If your Mommy tells you to do something, you have to do it." "If you get punched, you should punch back. If they hit you hard, you should hit them hard."

Piaget termed the principle behind such evaluations of moral responsibility crude equality or "sheer equality in all its brutality." It is the eye-for-an-eye approach, simple, straightforward, and admitting no exceptions. Five-year-old Angela's world is viewed in black-and-white terms. People are either all good or all bad. Nuances and complexities have no part in this thinking. This simple understanding of morality gives way as she gets older. At about ten years old, Piaget noted, a child sets forgiveness above revenge, not out of weakness but because "there is no end" to revenge. Her understanding of morality starts to encompass considerations of the future. Morality moves from the here and now to the then and maybe. By adolescence, her sense of justice also takes into consideration motive and context. Now Angela understands that someone may do something illegal out of desperation or cheat on a test because of great pressure from home to not fail a class.

Say Angela's parents take their three children to see *Les Miserable*. Seth, five, thinks that Jean Vol Jean should be punished for stealing a loaf of bread. Marie, ten, thinks that he should be forgiven for what he does, because hounding him simply leads to further problems. Angela, fifteen, is able to understand that he did nothing wrong to begin with.

Parents often find that their young children will present a rigid moral code, then do something else. Seth might assure his father he understands the rules by saying, "Taking a cookie without asking is wrong. Children shouldn't do that." But as soon as he is alone, he stares at the cookie jar, his mouth watering, until he can't stand it any longer and takes the cookie. What a little hypocrite! we think. What a bald-faced liar! How does Piaget explain this commonplace occurrence? He notes that we cannot expect consistency from children until they understand why moral rules are worth following. Until they can grasp the reasons behind the rules, it is the fear of punishment that motivates children to follow them. Seth doesn't understand them. A psychologist would say he hasn't internalized the rules. Taking in rules as one's own can happen only a little later in life.

Before internalization takes place, morality lacks roots. So Seth's parents leave the kitchen, and his desire to satisfy his sweet tooth becomes too strong to resist. He does what he wants (rather than the moral thing) because he is afraid of being punished. This type of morality Piaget calls "heteronomous," meaning that the rules come from outside oneself.

As long as your child is at the level of heteronomous morality, you shouldn't be surprised that she may act in a thoroughly appropriate way at home but occasionally behave in a destructive way elsewhere. It isn't that she forgets the rules when she leaves the house or that she thinks the rules are different in different places. Rather it is that she is good at home because of the fear of punishment. She is simply incapable of generalizing the rule from one context to the other.

In contrast to this phase stands the autonomous phase during which the motivation for moral behavior feels as though it came from within. Beginning at about twelve years of age, a child chooses the right thing not out of fear of being punished or to get something back in return. Angela doesn't take what isn't hers, not because she's afraid that she'll be caught or because others will think she's a bad girl if she does, but because she has a moral sense—a conscience—that guides her. This phase of reasoning resembles the ethical dictum that is found in religions through the world. To treat others as one would want to be treated in return overrules egocentric impulses. This isn't tit-for-tat thinking but something more mature: the ability to imagine oneself in the place of another. It is to imagine standing in another's shoes, seeing the world from someone else's perspective, a capacity that comes only with age.

To illustrate the point, Robert Kegan asked six-year-old children about the golden rule. Many could recite the rule accurately: Do unto others as you would have them do unto you. However, when he asked the same children what the rule tells them to do if someone hits them, their answers missed the spirit of the maxim. "Hit them back," they said. "Do unto others like they do unto you." Young children couldn't grasp the *meaning* of the maxim. They lacked the ability to understand the reason for the rule.

However, children's reasoning abilities don't always fall into neat categories. It's as though the physically maturing child were clumsy at one task but graceful in another. So the thinking about what's right or wrong is sometimes a mixture of contradictory reasons for making a moral judgment. Here is part of an interview Piaget conducted with Constance, age seven:

PIAGET: *Let's pretend that you are the mummy. You have two little girls. One of them breaks fifteen cups as she is coming into the dining room, the other breaks one cup as she is trying to get some jam while you are not there. Which of them would you punish more severely?*
CONSTANCE: *The one who broke the fifteen cups. . . .*
PIAGET: *Have you ever broken anything?*
CONSTANCE: *A cup.*
PIAGET: *How?*
CONSTANCE: *I wanted to wipe it, and I let it drop.*
PIAGET: *What else have you broken?*

CONSTANCE: Another time, a plate.

PIAGET: How?

CONSTANCE: I took it to play with.

PIAGET: Which was the naughtier thing to do?

CONSTANCE: The plate, because I oughtn't have taken it.

PIAGET: And how about the cup?

CONSTANCE: That was less naughty because I wanted to wipe it.

PIAGET: Which were you punished most for, the cup or the plate?

CONSTANCE: For the plate.

PIAGET: Listen, I am going to tell you two more stories. A little girl is wiping the cups. She is putting them away, wiping them with a cloth, and she broke five cups. Another little girl is playing with some plates. She breaks a plate. Which of them is naughtier?

CONSTANCE: The girl who broke the five cups.

The contradiction between reciting a moral rule and acting on the rule is familiar to all parents. But such disparities between saying and doing shouldn't upset us. It isn't that young children are willful in their responses. They don't even know what they are doing. It is like the child who can sing song lyrics without understanding what he is saying. ("Row, row, row your boat / Gently down the stream / Merrily, merrily, merrily, merrily / Life is buttering the dream," my young son used to sing.) Young children are literally incapable of understanding any better. Only with maturity can they stand apart, outside themselves, imagine themselves as another person and then make judgments about behavior while being aware of the complexity of what it means to be that person. I discussed some of these ideas in the section "Feelings" regarding the inherent capacity to feel for another person. The difference between this later capacity to see things from another's point of view and the earlier impulse of empathy is that toddlers do not distinguish between themselves and others. The feeler and what was being felt are identical.

For infants, perception and the perceiver are one and the same. It is as though another's pain were literally the infant's own rather than being *like* her own. Only later in life can children identify with another's feelings without confusing those feelings with their own. As toddlers mature into children, they begin to differentiate themselves from their surroundings.

A major contribution of Piaget's work is in making clear that just as children develop physically in a particular order (for example, first sitting up, then crawling, and finally walking), there is a definite direction in which children's reasoning ability develops. One component of cognitive development is that of making moral judgments.

American psychologist Lawrence Kohlberg elaborated and refined Piaget's work, accepting the idea that moral thinking grows in a particular direction and that this growth is natural to human beings. This is not to say that the outcome is inevitable. Sometimes development is arrested; sometimes it is fostered by new and favorable conditions. For example, in the last several generations children have been taller than their parents. Nothing has changed in our genes. It has been a matter of improved nutrition and fewer childhood diseases. In other words, the potential for growth is available to everyone—everything else being equal—but external conditions can either stunt that growth or promote it.

Although Piaget confined his observations to Swiss children, Kohlberg broadened the examination to include children from around the world. Since Kohlberg's initial study in the late 1950s, innumerable studies have been done. Most have confirmed his hypothesis that there is a natural tendency for moral judgments to develop in stages and that those stages unfold in sequence. A person can no more move from stage 1 reasoning to stage 4 by skipping stages 2 and 3 than he can grow from four feet tall to five feet tall by skipping the eleven inches in between. Kohlberg used the terminology of stages, conjuring an image much like steps on a staircase. Although sometimes the changes from one way of thinking to another can be abrupt, it is more helpful to think of the stages as stops along a highway. Between the various stages, a person may employ a mix of concepts and motivations, until the next step fully replaces the one before. Talking to a child who combines two phases at one time can be exasperating. "Can't you see that you have just said one thing, now another?" we are tempted to ask. No, she can't.

A word of explanation about the relation between age and stage is called for. Moral maturation, like all other kinds, occurs not in clockwork fashion but fluidly. Some children reach a stage much sooner than others. What's more, not everyone reaches the final stages. For a variety of reasons, many of which are discussed in this book, moral growth is stunted. It also happens, though rarely, that someone regresses to an earlier stage of thinking.

With this in mind, here is a summary of the stages, described by Kohlberg and largely accepted by moral psychologists:

Stage 1: Punishment–Obedience, (One to Eight Years Old)

The first stage of development is the most concrete form of thinking. Rules are obeyed to avoid punishment. What is right is what authority says is right. And who is that authority? As one child told Kohlberg, "The father is the boss because he's bigger." The world is understood in self-centered terms, and there is confusion or the inability to recognize that other's needs may be different from one's own. Only as the child begins to recognize herself as someone apart from others, is it possible to make different kinds of moral judgments.

Stage 1 thinking is thoroughly self-centered. At this point, children are practical, calculating right and wrong like little accountants balancing their books and paying attention to the bottom line. Can I get away with it? Who can punish me? A child at stage 1 is after as much as she can grab while avoiding as much pain as possible. It's as if the child were running around shouting, "I'm number one, I'm number one!" Actually, the child couldn't understand the implications of such a statement (that there are others who are number two, and so on) because the child's mind can't conceive that other people have needs and wants that matter as much as her own. The child can't understand what it means not to be who she is and not to want what she wants. The only reason a small child goes along with a rule contrary to her own desires is that someone bigger has commanded it. If you ask a young girl if she has a sister and she says yes, ask her if her sister has a sister. She will say no. This is a rudimentary understanding of both the physical and the social world; it is the only perspective she is able to grasp. At this stage, morality is understood as totally externally oriented. I'll only do it because others tell me to, and if I don't I'll get punished.

Stage 2: Let's Make a Deal (Eight to Twelve Years Old)

Children move on to the next style of reasoning (stage 2) somewhere between the ages of eight and twelve. What makes judgments here different from before is that stage 2 is the beginning of taking other people's interests into account. At this stage, children are nice so they can get along. It is tit-for-tat thinking. I'll be nice to Chris; then Chris will be nice to me. I won't lie to Pat, so Pat won't lie to me. At this stage, children discover a phrase that haunts nearly every household in which there is more than one child: It's not fair! He has more candy than I do; she is allowed to stay up later than me; his piece of cake is bigger than mine, ad nauseam. All explanations about justice appear to fall on deaf ears. It all comes down to the same thing, It's not fair!

Appeals to authority may stop the whining, but it doesn't soothe the aggrieved conscience. To the child crying foul, all explanations are rationalizations. What is fair is obvious. Being fair is being equal and equal means the same. A slogan such as "Each according to his needs" is incomprehendible to the child. Benevolence and equity haven't yet entered into his thinking. He can no more reason with these factors than a child first learning to add and subtract can understand division and multiplication.

To understand what is going on, it is useful to know a little about stage 2 thinking. Although more abstract than the previous stage, it is still specific and applied to particular situations. The social world is unbending and exacting. Robert Kegan illustrates this type of reasoning by relating an experience he had as a seventh-grade teacher. In one of his classes he had his students read a short story about a boy their age who played a baseball game. Marty was a rotten ball player and hoped that he could get through a game without having to field a ball. But on this day, he has to make the key play of the game. Flailing about, he chases the ball only to muff the play and lose the game for his team. Poor Marty. His friends ridicule his performance. Then one day a new kid moves into the neighborhood, someone more clumsy than Marty. When sides are chosen, for the first time Marty isn't the last picked. And sure enough the new kid finds himself in the same position as Marty did earlier in the summer: A ball is coming his way, he runs this way and that, misses the ball, and loses the game for the team. He walks back to the dugout a dejected, pathetic figure. Humiliating taunts are heaped on his drooping shoulders, the jeering led by none other than Marty.

So, the teacher asks his class, what do you think the moral of the story is? Kegan summarizes his pupils' responses this way, "The story is saying that people may be mean to you and push you down and make you feel crummy and stuff, but it's saying things aren't really all that bad because eventually you'll get your chance to push someone down and then you'll be on top." Kegan thought that his students must have been putting him on. It wasn't the moral that he wanted them to relate. He asked them if they thought that what Marty had done was really okay. Here are a few of their responses: "It was more than okay; it was the right thing to do." "It was the only thing to do." "Look, we were six graders last year, right?—the oldest in the school. We pushed the little kids around. Now we're the little kids and we're getting pushed around. Wait till we're seniors! Fair is fair!"

Kegan's initial exasperation at the students' insensitive responses gave way to new understanding and insight as he placed their comments in the framework developed by Kohlberg. Instead of hearing their answers as immoral, Kegan now understood them through the theory of moral development. Students were using different levels of moral reasoning. Kegan realized that it was unrealistic to expect his pupils, who were still maturing, to think as he did. In fact, when he applied Kohlberg's stage theory to his pupils, he understood them as expressing sentiments appropriate to their age. Kohlberg says that for this age, morality means an equal exchange. Something was done to you, now you do it to someone else. So the pupils weren't immoral or amoral. In fact, they were little moralists, knowing precisely what was right and anticipating the hand of justice. They had no doubt that Marty's teammates had mistreated him. They had done him wrong. They also had no qualms about evaluating Marty. He was wrong for what he did to the new kid. But the students couldn't condemn anyone, because they were all doing what comes naturally. That's the deal. Big kids always pick on little ones, and when little ones grow up they will get their chance to pick on those coming up behind them. The students could understand how others felt, Marty first, then the new kid. What they couldn't do is to make the connection between the various characters in the story and understand all the feelings simultaneously.

Stage 3. Good Boy/Nice Girl (Eleven to Eighteen Years Old)

No sooner have children integrated stage 2 reasoning than they begin to incorporate a wider way of thinking and making ethical judgments. In stage 3, children begin to form real relationships, not only with the family but with friends, schoolmates, and neighbors. At stage 3, the child is very much tuned in to other people and she cares a great deal about what others think of her. She is beginning to take on the rules and expectations of the people to whom she is related. She identifies strongly with the groups that she is a part of, and group loyalty becomes a dominant feature. She wants to be thought of as a good person by those in her group.

Now Mario's sense of the right thing isn't determined by the fear of punishment, nor is it governed by getting what he thinks he deserves. Rather it is looking good in the eyes of others. He won't cheat, because he knows that good boys aren't cheaters. Mutual affection, gratitude, and concern for another's approval are uppermost in Mario's thinking. There is much caring of individuals for each other at this stage.

This level of development has its limitations. First, it works well for small groups, such as family and friends. It rests on a concern about what others think about us. I know you, you know me, and I want you to think well of me. I want you to like me. I want to fit in. But what about the bigger world, where people don't know each other personally? Andrew will be fiercely loyal to his family and friends, but why should he be concerned about strangers? The second limitation is that there is a strong tendency toward conformity. If I am concerned about pleasing other people, I'm not going to go out of my way to think for myself or do much that is going to get me into trouble with the group. Most of the time when we say that an infant is a good baby, what we mean is that she doesn't fuss much. A content baby is a good baby. But it is obvious that contentment or conformity isn't identical with goodness. Making bullies conform to a higher standard is a good thing, but making decent people conform to injustices is obviously an awful thing.

Stage 4. Law and Order (Sixteen to Twenty-One Years Old)

There are good reasons why stage 3 thinking generally gives way to stage 4. Let's look at the golden rule, first through the lens of stage 2. If you ask children at this stage what the rule means, they say something like, "You should hit him back since he has hit you." And why should someone follow the golden rule? It's because you get back what you give. Stage 3 reasons that if you hit someone, he won't like you.

At stage 4, the reasons for the golden rule differ. Because you are now capable of putting yourself in someone's position, you can imagine what it's like to be the other person. Therefore, you begin to factor her needs into your decision making. At this stage, children can imagine what it is like to be another person even if they have had no personal experience of her situation. Our relationships with other people no longer turn on exchanges but on an ideal of equity. So we help, not because we expect to be helped in return but because society functions best when there are stable relationships.

The mutual understanding of small groups (the defining characteristic of stage 3) simply can't work in a larger network. Although Scott may get along fine with his schoolmates in high school without a system of laws because they all know each other, this can't happen when he is dealing with larger groups in which people who need to get along with each other may never, in fact, meet.

For the first time, a person is able to understand that society needs laws to function. Laws need to be fairly enforced, applying equally to those you know and those you don't. There is now an obligation to society as a whole. It is no longer doing the right thing to be a nice boy or good girl. It becomes clear that each person in society has a part to play, and the right thing to do is to make a contribution to society, group, or institution according to your role. So Scott may be class president and will want to fulfill that role by doing what a president is supposed to do, even if it means making some of his friends unhappy. His conscience won't allow him to play favorites. There is one problem here, though. Scott may carry out his duties a little harshly, carrying the letter of the law to the extreme. He won't let anyone get away with anything. "The rule's the rule," he may say, refusing to make even the smallest exception to a minor infraction.

Another limitation of this stage is that the child tends to think that everyone should follow the same laws. He makes no exceptions, not even for cultural differences. If there is a rule against wearing a hat in school, an observant Muslim shouldn't be allowed to cover her head.

Stage 5. Golden Rule (Over Eighteen Years Old)

Stage 5 is more flexible than the previous one. Laws are upheld because there is a sense that there is a social contract between members of a society and that we abide by laws for the welfare of all people and for the protection of all people's rights. In other words, rules are meant to benefit everyone and sometimes strict adherence to the rules can actually work against making a better society.

I can remember an incident from my own life when the distinction between these two stages began to dawn on me.

When I was a teenager, my friends wanted to play organized basketball but there was no local team for us to join. We found a league nearby but we needed institutional sponsorship. So we decided that under the umbrella of a nearby religious institution we would create a social club and the club in turn would sponsor the team. The only thing that they required of us is that the club live according to a set of bylaws that spelled out the rules and regulations. We didn't have rules like this for the park, so why did we need them now? That's what clubs do, we were told. Since none of us knew anything about bylaws, we were handed the boilerplate variety by our new adviser. And once we had them, we enforced them with a vengeance. I remember our saying things such as, "If you are going to be in this club, you better come to the meetings. If you don't pay your dues, you're going to be thrown out. If you miss more than two practices, you may as well hang up your sneakers. We can't let you get away with it. If everyone did that, we wouldn't have a club."

We elected officers, held meetings, collected dues, and arranged for dances. We had our club of good close friends—neighborhood basketball buddies. Everything was great. The halcyon days abruptly came to an end when a stranger wanted to join the club. We didn't accept his application. I told our adviser we didn't want him. Why, the adviser asked. I said that he didn't fit in; he wasn't our kind. "Hold on," Mr. Heller said, "it just isn't right to keep a person out like this."

We argued with Mr. Heller. It was our club, we could do whatever we wanted. The bylaws didn't say we had to take anyone who applied. We were sticking to the letter of the law. "True enough," Mr. Heller said. "But the point is, the club is meant for everyone. It isn't enough just to stick to the rules. You also have to live with the spirit behind the rules."

Our group eventually gave in, not because we agreed with what our adviser was saying, but because we wanted to play league basketball. We weren't yet at stage 5. If we had been, we would have been able to understand what Jesus, Martin Luther King Jr., and thousands of others did who challenged the law: Laws are meant for the welfare of all people and are upheld because they serve a common good. The spirit of the law is sometimes more important than the letter of the law.

*　　　*　　　*

Piaget's and Kohlberg's developmental theories provide us with a useful tool for understanding how children employ reason in making moral judgments. It helps know that the self-centered and inconsistent moral behavior we see in young children gradually gives way to a more encompassing, stable, and responsible view of themselves in relation to society. If we remember this, we will be less disappointed that our young children are selfish, and we don't need to be so hard on ourselves when our children assure us that they know the right thing to do but then do another. We aren't failures as moral teachers. "They are going through a stage," we might say, and we're right. The developmentalist theory tells us to be patient. Moral growth takes time. Of course, we knew that already. But it is good to have the evidence support our inclinations.

6.

Give Reasons Why You Approve or Disapprove of Your Children's Behavior

We often forget to tell a child why we approve of what he does. It's as though we take good behavior for granted. But your children need to learn why something was good just as much as why it was bad.

Your four-year-old has a fistful of pennies and her younger cousin is sobbing because he doesn't have any. At first she doesn't want to give him any but, after much prodding by you, she finally offers him one.

"That's good sharing," you say to your four-year-old. "It makes your cousin happy when you share with him."

When your child does the right thing, take the time to explain why it was right. This is more than simply reiterating the rule, such as "Sharing is good," but the reasons behind the rule, such as, "Sharing helps us get along with others." As your child gets older, the reasons you give can get more sophisticated. Try to keep a rough sketch of the stages of moral development in mind.

Most of the time, though, with young children we aren't praising them for something done properly but admonishing them for that which they shouldn't have done. One reason we spend so much time saying no is that young children simply can't tell the difference between danger and safety, appropriate and inappropriate social behavior. Another reason is that children are naturally curious and are frequently trying out new ways of behaving.

"Because you will get hurt if you run into the street," you

can say when Jennifer scoots out into the street. "I don't want you to get hurt."

At some point, after several responses, you will have to insist that the rule be followed even if Jennifer thinks the rule stinks and she fusses. Adults are protectors of children and, as such, have a moral responsibility to see that children are taken care of.

"I don't care if I get hurt," Jennifer insists.

"I do. And I said no, and that's the end of it!"

And it often is. Jennifer may nurse hurt feelings, she may be angry with you, but no matter. You had to do your job and you did, first, by telling her what the rule is and why and, second, by making sure that she obeyed the (reasonable) rule.

Kevin grabs the toy from Jennifer.

"Please, give that back to her," you say.

Kevin says nothing but hides the little horse behind his back.

"We have to learn how to share," we add.

But Kevin doesn't care about sharing. He wants the horse and for Jennifer to disappear.

So we add a little more. "You are making Jennifer unhappy. Everyone is happier when we share. You wouldn't want Jennifer to take away the horse when you have it, do you?"

Kevin may not understand what you're saying. He may be too immature. But he does know that you disapprove of what he has done. You are gently helping him move from stage 1 to stage 2 by letting him know that if he wants to be liked by you, he has to share. It may take years for him to get to that point, but you are doing your job by encouraging his growth in that direction.

In addition, he is also learning something significant for his long-term development as an ethical person. That is that there is a *reason* why he shouldn't take the horse away and that reason has to do with how it makes others feel and how people get along with one another. Although he may give in because you insist and are bigger than he, Kevin is learning that power also needs to have good reasons.

From the kind of answers you give, your children will learn either that rules are arbitrary and are to be followed because someone is bigger and stronger or that rules are important because there is a solid reason for the existence of the rule in the first place. If you explain the reason behind the rule to them, you are helping them move from one stage to the next.

7.

Provide Reasons for Rules You Want Your Children to Follow

Demanding behavior from Jennifer without giving reasons leads to trouble. Jennifer may comply, but she is also likely to become sullen and defiant in underhanded ways.

So Jennifer demands to know why she has to wait her turn. The question—a deserved challenge to your authority—requires a thoughtful answer. For Jennifer is setting out on the course of understanding the reasons behind the rules. If there is good reason for them, she will, at a later stage, accept the rules as her own and willingly live by them.

If there is no good reason for the rules we have, then, as adults, we have to rethink why we have the rule in the first place. This may seem to undermine parental or adult authority. Authority *is* essential but the rules that authority conveys have to be based in something sound. By giving reasons for the rules we expect children to follow, we aren't undermining our authority. Quite the opposite. In the long run it confers on adults an authority that is deserved because the behavior we expect serves a good purpose.

By giving reasons for the rules we ask our children to follow, we are helping them move from one stage of development to the next. Of course, they won't always understand the explanation. They may be too young to grasp the significance of what we are saying. No matter. They will get something over time. It is important to remind ourselves over and over: This will take time.

In the not too distant past (and sadly, for many, even today) adults thought that children learned morality through one of three ways: shame, guilt, or fear.

Spare the rod and spoil the child, is the adage. The rod doesn't have to be a real stick. Making a child feel guilty or ashamed has the same withering effect. Children can be cowered into good behavior.

At least we think that's what happens. Actually, we don't achieve real moral behavior this way but something very different: obedience. For it is only when a child understands *why* it is right to do good that she will become a *real* ethical person.

A person may do the right thing for the wrong reasons. This happens all the time. We may stop at a red light not because we think that traffic lights save lives but because we are afraid that a police car is around the corner.

In the same way, an obedient person may do the right thing because the person he is listening to is telling him the right thing, and this isn't a problem—as long as life presents no conflicts. However, as adults we know that sometimes we are forced to make a choice between what we want and what others want of us, between what others want us to do and what we think is the moral thing to do. Those who were rescuers of Jews in Nazi Europe found themselves in exactly this situation.

8.

Encourage Your Children to Play with Children of Various Ages

As much as we parents like to think that we are central to how our children think about morality, the fact is that much of moral growth takes place without us. A major stimulus to moral reasoning is other children, on the playground, in the home, wherever they play together.

Children learn to reason about all sorts of things—about the nature of time and space, about numbers, and so forth. Moral reasoning is part of that process that unfolds as children grow older. But it is also different from other kinds of reasoning. Most reasoning can be learned through formal teaching, but moral thinking is largely stimulated by encountering real-life dilemmas posed by the necessity of getting along with others. It is because Kevin and Jennifer can't have the same toy at the same time that they *must* find a solution to their little drama.

Moral intelligence and other forms of intelligence aren't identical. IQ scores measure one kind of reasoning skills but don't measure ethical sensibilities any more than they measure, for example, musical ability. These various forms of intelligence explain why someone may be a math whiz but socially inept or a musical genius but morally indifferent.

You often want to intervene to stop children from quarreling by solving their problems for them. Sometimes this is necessary—to prevent harm, to stop bullies, to preserve our own sanity and peace of mind. On the whole, children learn best by sorting out problems among themselves. From the point of view of moral development, children are better off arranging their own games, making their own rules, and enforcing those rules by themselves than they are participating in sports in which adults officiate and settle all disputes.

The fear is that children won't resolve their problems in an acceptable way. They will develop a *Lord of the Flies* society, we think, in which selfishness rules. The concern isn't really well founded, given that they come from homes that foster feelings and intelligence. Moral reasoning develops more or less spontaneously as children find themselves in social situations that present moral conflicts. When children cannot resolve the conflict at hand, they search for different responses that will work. This is the spur to development.

Interestingly, children advance by being exposed to those who are slightly more advanced than they are. It's as though awareness arose because someone was holding out a light just a little in front. A five-year-old can't understand a lecture on social justice ("There are people not as fortunate as you, Kevin."), but they do get the point from an eight-year-old about sharing ("If you share one of your toys," the older child explains, "then Mommy will buy you a new one.").

So, from the point of view of moral development, children are better off on the sandlot than in Little League; they are better off in fantasy play with other children than in educational classes that set specific goals and rules determined by adults. The relatively unstructured play that arises spontaneously from children spending time together allows them to develop their skills in solving social problems. The best an adult can do is to encourage children to be children, fostering social gatherings at which children of various ages get together and letting them work out their own problems about how to get along—provided they don't hurt one another.

9.

Engage Your Children in Reflective Discussions by Asking Open-Ended Questions

Talk to your children. Have real conversations with them. Find out what is on their minds. Get them to reflect on what they are doing. Today's ethical people were once children who were encouraged to think for themselves. They weren't told what to do as much as asked to think about what they were doing.

There can be no prep classes in morality. You can't hand anyone the right answer. Memorizing the Ten Commandments isn't any more likely to make a truthful person than the person who has never heard of the commandments but has been taught to be sensitive to the lives of others and encouraged to think things through for herself.

I understand wanting to teach children morality by giving them a program to follow. But we simply don't get ethical people that way. Programs that stress a set of virtues to be memorized, such as telling the truth, being loyal, and so forth, miss the mark. There is no harm done by posting rules of good behavior on a bulletin board, but we are fooling ourselves if we think that children who can recite them accurately will be good children. The limitation of such an approach is that it often comes from the top down and has the same shortcomings as any coaching does when it tells people what to do rather than showing by example and letting them learn by doing.

Students who are best at moral reasoning "are those who love to learn, seek new challenges, enjoy intellectually stimulating environments, who are reflective, who make plans and set goals, who take risks, who see themselves in the larger social contexts of history and institutions and broad cultural trends, who take responsibility for themselves and their environs," James Rest writes.

How did these students acquire such attitudes? They received "encouragement to continue their education and development," Rest notes. "They profit from stimulating and challenging environments, and from social milieus that support their work, interest them, and reward their accomplishments. . . . This pattern is one of general social/cognitive development."

A study conducted by Sprinthall and Scott of high school students concludes that moral reasoning is fostered when a three-pronged approach is taken. First, older children tutored younger students. This was the point made in chapter 8 about how children learn best from someone who is slightly more advanced than they are. Second, the students read articles on psychology. This seems to have stimulated a sense of identification with other people, even those who may not be like themselves. And third, the students participated in seminars designed to elicit thoughtful responses. These classes didn't try to teach content matter as such. Rather, students were asked questions that encouraged them to think for themselves. Because there were no exact right answers, students didn't worry about memorizing or cramming or doing those other mind-numbing things that students are often expected to do. Those who were exposed to all three approaches improved their ability to make mature moral judgments.

Something similar can be done with even young children. When you read your son a story, conclude by asking him open-ended questions. These are questions that require something more than a yes or no response. They are meant to engage the child so that he is encouraged to think about the meaning of the story for himself.

In my book of fables for children, *Love Your Neighbor,* I end each story with an open-ended question. Here are summaries of two of the stories.

One day Lola buys the most beautiful bird she has ever seen. She loves the bird. Whenever she looks at its gorgeous plumage, her heart soars with happiness. Whenever she listens to its lilting song, she is overcome with joy.

However, one day she notices that its feathers have begun to fade and its song has grown weak. She realizes that her bird is dying and she doesn't know what to do.

"On the other side of the ocean," the bird said to her as she leaned close to the cage, "there is a bird who will tell you what to do."

Lola sailed across the sea until she found the bird. She listened to his advice and returned home.

"I'm sorry, dear bird," she said, as she opened the door to the cage. The bird took flight and as it flew away she could hear its beautiful song once again and its feathers were as bright as a rainbow.

"Good bye, dear bird," Lola said as she wiped away her tears.

Question: Do you think Lola was happy or sad to see the bird fly away?

Nicholas and his son, Victor, were two stubborn camels. One day Nicholas told his son that his Aunt Tamisha was coming for a visit. She was on her way elsewhere, so she could stay for only a short while.

The day that Aunt Tamisha was to arrive, Victor went to town to buy fruits and nuts in honor of the visit.

On the way back, just as he was about to pass through the city's narrow gate, he met another camel ready to pass through the gate in the other direction.

Victor demanded that the other camel move aside but he refused to do so, claiming that he was there first. So the two camels stood there all day, both refusing to budge. Finally, after the sun set, Victor was able to squeeze past the other camel who, by now, had fallen asleep.

Victor ran home to meet his aunt.

"I'm sorry, Victor," his father said. "But Aunt Tamisha needed to catch the evening train. She left more than an hour ago. Sorry you have missed her."

Question: What do you think Victor could have done instead of standing in the gate for so long?

These kind of stories as moral education are more effective than the traditional fables that end with someone being punished and with the application of a ready-made and handed-over aphorism. A typical Aesop fable concludes with a comment such as "Honesty is the best policy." Honesty may well be the best policy, but children will come to that conclusion on their own through enough reflection and observation.

Remember, children progress through the stages of moral judgment by being placed in situations that require solutions. Understanding, insight, and appreciation that is gained through personal effort is more likely to become part of who they are than the lessons learned by rote or taken because someone else has given the answer.

Left on their own, children don't need encouragement to ask questions. *Why* must be the most commonly used word in a young child's vocabulary. But somewhere along the line, many children are taught to keep quiet, not ask too many questions and accept what an adult has told them. Too many adults just want to be left alone or simply want their children to do what they are told, no questions asked, quenching the fire of inquiry.

10.

Promote Independent Thinking

Despots and bullies insist on conformity in thinking. They don't want anyone asking questions. But without independence of thought there is no real moral life. This is what Aristotle meant in his ethical theory when he said that ethics begins in choice. When we choose to do what we do, rather than doing it because we are afraid or because we will get something from it in return or because we want to be liked, then we have the beginning of real ethics.

This is the difference between the first three stages of moral development and what comes after. In stages 1 through 3 moral thinking goes along with convention and is, in some sense, pre-ethical. After that point, moral thinking stands above the pressures of individuals or groups, and the child grasps the importance of an independent standard, one embedded in law or in a universal principle.

No one starts out thinking independently. We reach that point only by going through the stages of obedience (stage 1), let's make a deal (stage 2), and good boy/nice girl (stage 3) that I spoke about before. Of course, children have their own opinions long before reaching stage 4. Those opinions usually revolve around likes and dislikes. Jennifer wanting an ice-cream cone when we want her to eat her vegetables is not so much independent thinking as an expression of desire. When young children express their opinions, they may be tuned in to their own feelings, but insisting on acting on those feelings may not be wise: It may be only stubbornness.

The importance of recognizing the developmental process in moral thinking is that we can't expect young children to think for themselves about many things. They aren't capable and so may put themselves in danger. Independent thinking comes with maturity.

Yet there are steps that can be taken to help your child reach the goal. Unfortunately, there are children who are thwarted from ever thinking for themselves. This can happen for a couple of reasons. One is that doing the right thing may be unpopular. And being less than popular can also mean being unhappy. Everyone wants to be included, wants to be liked.

As parents, we have to make a basic decision about how we will raise our children. Are we raising them to be happy or do we want them to be good? In the best of all worlds, they can be both. Sometimes, though, a choice needs to be made.

The second reason that independent thinking isn't always encouraged is because, deep down, some adults really don't want children to make up their minds about important matters. We may be afraid of losing them to another world, a different way of life, one that excludes us. If our children made up their own minds, if we let them choose what they think is best, they may choose the wrong thing—maybe something unethical or self-destructive. So we tell Kevin and Jennifer that they are free to choose their own friends when they are teenagers, but then discourage them from hanging out with those who aren't to our liking. Our children may even choose to reject the things that are most precious to us, such as our religion. Their loves, commitments, and passions may not be the same as our own.

This is a risk. Our child may go her own way, on a path that we wouldn't have chosen for her. But if we raise our children well, it is far more likely that they will love us for having given them a life they can call their own and for having been given a conscience to live by. That love transcends whatever differences may otherwise separate us.

Someone once remarked that every day he asks himself three questions: Have I helped others? Have I been a true friend? Have I passed on to others what I have learned?

These are wonderful questions that promote independent thinking, as well as moral sensibilities. They are good questions to ask yourself; they are good questions to introduce to your children.

Self-Esteem

Self-Respect Is a Prerequisite to Acting Morally

> Civilization is a method of living and an attitude of equal respect for all people.
> —JANE ADDAMS, in *Democracy and Social Ethics*

Through my work with the human rights organization Amnesty International, I became interested in meeting people who had been prisoners of conscience, people imprisoned on the basis of their beliefs. I wanted to know their stories and how they survived jail, torture, and separation from their families. I met Eduardo and Natasha Becerra soon after they arrived in the United States as political refugees. He had been an officer in the Chilean Air Force and she was a schoolteacher. When the military overthrew the Chilean civilian government in 1973, Eduardo was arrested, imprisoned, and tortured because he supported the overthrown democratic government.

Eduardo was in jail for five months before the military came for Natasha. She, too, was taken from her children and detained. Her jailers threatened her with torture. The soldiers told her they would shoot Eduardo if she didn't confess to being a spy. Their threats had the opposite effect than the intended one: Natasha summoned the strength to resist the pressure, a strength she didn't know she possessed. Instead of caving in to their threats, she defended Eduardo's good name and his character, refusing to say what wasn't true. Unable to get Natasha to denounce her husband, the military released them both.

I asked Eduardo and Natasha how they had survived such indignities. Natasha spoke for them both, "I think we kept sane and strong and continue to love life because we believe in human beings. Whenever I looked around me—when Eduardo was being held in secret, when I was being held—I always saw some smiling eyes, a hand, something that made me believe. We know that there are a few bad people, but there are also good people. You cannot let the bad few spoil everything." Then, echoing Anne Frank, she added, "Life is good."

Natasha and Eduardo Becerra, like the Holocaust rescuers in Germany, had no illusions about the world. They had seen their country's democratic government toppled in a coup, they had lost their jobs, suffered arrest and torture, and had to abandon their homeland. Yet through all this, they believed they could influence their destiny.

People like the Becerras get us to look at self-esteem, for there is a connection between a willingness to assume responsibility for the course of one's own life and self-esteem. Those who feel they have some control over events around them also tend to be people who have high self-esteem. The relationship isn't perfect, but it's close. Consistently, psychologists find when a person values herself, likes herself, accepts and respects herself, then she is also likely to believe that she has the ability to direct her own life.

For the Becerras and others even in the most appalling circumstances, there is a shred of control. A colleague of mine who for forty years was the spiritual leader of the Ethical Culture Society in the Bronx, tells me that even when the Nazis condemned him to death because of his work in the Dutch underground, he never felt completely helpless. "Several of us had made a vow," Les Spetter said. "When—it was never 'if'—the guards would come to murder us, we weren't going to go like sheep. We were going to take some of them with us." Americans liberated Spetter's camp before he needed to put his plan into action.

Stalin's Soviet Union couldn't tolerate an independent spirit such as that of the poet Osip Mandelstam. After many arrests, he was finally sent to a Gulag in remote Siberia. The government silenced him, censored and removed his books, and limited his audience to fellow inmates. But Mandelstam continued to compose, reciting his poems to other prisoners. After his disappearance and death, his poetry appeared, passed by word of mouth. Fragments of his work summed up his defiance and hope, tattered and thin as it was. "You left me my lips," he wrote, "And they shape words / Even in silence."

Self-Determination

Psychologists have looked at the degree to which people believe they can influence and are responsible for events in their lives. People who believe that they can "shape words even in silence" have what social scientists call an internal locus of control. Those who attribute events in their lives to such things as fate or luck—forces over which they feel they have no control— have an external locus of control.

There is strong evidence supporting the idea that there is a relationship between internal locus of control and self-esteem. For example, in one university study involving black male adolescents, researchers Tashakori and Thompson found those who had higher self-esteem also had a higher internal locus of control. Another study, by Taisir Abdallah, conducted in Saudi Arabia involving 300 male college students, reached the same conclusion. These two studies echo numerous others that make the same point: There is a consistent correlation between self-esteem and self-efficacy (locus of control).

There is little doubt that the family is an important factor in linking self-esteem and locus of control. Nancy Chubb and Carl Fertman explored the differences between ninth graders who had a sense of belonging in their families and those who did not. Children who felt they belonged had a high degree of self-esteem and a strong sense of self-determination. The factors that influenced both were parents who had an interest in the lives and activities of their children and warm, protective, and nurturing homes. Parents from these homes both respected their children and provided them with solid emotional support.

The reason that your interest in your child's activities is so important in terms of self-esteem is because the underlying message your child receives is: I care about you and I respect the life that you have. What interests you matters to me. You matter. When your child experiences your benevolent interest, she knows that you won't let her go too far. And when she has your attention, she need not engage in outrageous (sometimes antisocial) behavior to get it.

All this presumes a proper attitude that falls somewhere between disinterest on one hand and overinvolvement on the other. Parents' intrusiveness and excessive control cause many problems. Somewhere between the poles of "you're on your own" and "tell me everything" is the encouragement to be oneself without being alone. Becoming entangled in family life hinders and discourages critical and independent thinking, the very qualities necessary to lead a moral life when life situations are ambiguous or when the group itself is engaged in immoral actions.

The evidence showing the importance of particular qualities in a family is overwhelming. Children who believe their parents nourish them emotionally, who believe their parents care for them as people, have high self-esteem. They also believe they can control events in their lives.

Expectations

Parental involvement seems to be the key to building self-esteem. Children with high self-esteem more often have parents who are actively involved in their lives. (This factor seems to be more important for boys than for girls.) High self-esteem is related to a parent's acceptance of her child's strengths and weaknesses. There is an important point here. Cheerleading isn't the same as providing self-esteem. Self-esteem is promoted more from someone who acts as a good coach. Pom-poms wave, whatever the players do, but the good coach points out what needs improvement and encourages the players to fulfill their potential. Cheerleaders say, "You're great." Good coaches say, "That was good. Now let's try it again."

This is a balanced approach to acceptance. It means that the child is seen for who he truly is. To be known in this manner is to be respected, for it says that you are a real person, not a model or an image or some hoped-for but unrealized child.

Parents who are clear about expectations and limits tend to have children with high self-esteem. The expectations, however, must be both realistic and slightly out of reach. Expectations are important, because they let the child know that certain behaviors are desirable and others are unacceptable. Setting expectations that are slightly out of reach challenges the child to develop skills. The child's self-esteem is then based on a sense of worthiness that issues from mastery of his environment. This then leads to the belief that it is possible to control the events in his life. Expectations that are unrealistic, though, are detrimental. Persistent failure doesn't produce confidence but its opposite. Eventually, the child gives up, knowing that no matter what he does, he is doomed to defeat. What's more, parents who have very high expectations of their children often aren't as concerned with their child's self-esteem as their own. They want their children to shine where they have been dull. Seldom does this lead to healthy self-esteem. If the child fails, she suffers the humiliation of having disappointed her parents. If she succeeds, she has an unrealistic view of life, thinking that the world turns on her. At the extremes, such a child becomes either self-centered or depressed.

Unconsciously projecting one's own desires on a child is, unfortunately, all too common. Psychologist Chris Mruk summarizes the parental factors influencing self-esteem as "the prevailing attitudes are those of involvement (but not smothering), acceptance (but not at the price of indulgence), firmness (but not rigidity), being democratic (but not simplistically so), and doing so consistently (most of the time). Being valued and treated in these ways appears to be self-esteem enhancing across the board."

M. Deborah Hyde-Rowan, a black neurosurgeon, reflects on her life as a child in an essay in the book *Courage of Conviction*. She writes, "Growing up in Mississippi, riding in the back of a bus, using water fountains marked 'colored,' entering the back door of restaurants and medical clinics, and contending with a society that tried to tell me that I was inferior, I never lost the feeling given to me by my family that I was special." Her mother, her grandmother, and others told her that she "was somebody and could be or do anything on this earth if I would only study hard and keep faith in God." The encouragement she received from those close to her became a self-fulfilling prophecy: Because they believed in her, she believed in herself; because she believed in herself, she succeeded.

We are what we think others think we are, according to George Herbert Mead. What we hear about ourselves from others—what we *think* they are saying—is what we expect them to say about us. If we have been encouraged and supported as children, we tend to hear what other people say about us as positive. But if we have been abused or ridiculed, we detect a cutting edge in their words. A child who has been trusted and found the world trustworthy likely matures into an adult who believes what others say. Isaac Bashevis Singer once said that a knife can either cut a piece of bread or kill. Some of us see a knife and think of sliced bread, others are reminded of murder. The way we interpret things is consistent with the way we have been taught the world works.

Our experiences structure the world for us, serving as a filter that says "This is important" and "That is irrelevant." We are surrounded by too much sensory input to take everything in. Other people like us, they dislike us, they are indifferent, they are critical. We don't—and can't—accept everything that we hear. Neither do we hear everything that is said. We take in that information that is consistent with our existing self-image and we reject that which contradicts it. People tell us what they think of us in many different ways. They smile or scowl, they approach us at a party or overlook us, they give us a raise or pass us over. Their responses—and more important, how we interpret those responses—reinforce and shore up the picture we already have formed of ourselves. The feedback reinforces the way in which we know ourselves, either as competent and worthy people or as incompetent and unworthy oafs.

Competence

Self-esteem is enhanced by competence because it leads to control over the environment. A person who is competent can, at least in some measure, compose her own life.

A sense of competency can start with small projects, such as the one undertaken by my foster daughter, Millie. Millie is now a grown woman; she lived with us during her teenage years. She grew up in an emotionally violent household in the south Bronx, in what we today label a dysfunctional family. School was a refuge for her, a place to get away from drunkenness and neglect.

Millie was in the sixth grade when her teacher selected her and five other children to join the school's new gardening club. The children were told they could choose from many different types of flowers and vegetables and were shown pictures of what the seeds and bulbs would become. They were given paper and art supplies and told to plan.

"What initially came into my mind was the school, my safety zone," says Millie, "so I decided I would write out the name of the school—PS 23—in flowers." Millie chose tulips. "It seemed to me that tulips would be able to spell the name best," she says.

The class went outside one cool October afternoon. The children had been given basic instructions on how to break the ground and how to plant. Millie tilled the earth and planted her bulbs.

She wondered about her tulips throughout the winter and would check to see if something had happened. When it started to get really cold and snowy she feared they would never pop up. Finally, in early spring, Millie noticed a change.

"When I saw the cracking of the earth, I was delighted," she says. "I knew then that something was going to come up." Millie's flowers grew tall and bloomed bright yellow. At the end of the year, at sixth-grade graduation, Millie won a medal for the best garden.

Millie says that the gardening experience taught her that the ground was more than a place to play. It also was the first time in her life that she was able to plan something from beginning to the end and to experience the process. "I learned about patience and hope," she says.

As the studies of Holocaust rescuers show us, the perception of yourself as powerful enough to influence your own circumstances is a prerequisite for altruistic behavior. Another source of self-esteem comes from acceptance. Being related to others, being part of a larger whole provides meaning and purpose to living, just as a note has a purpose in a song but can never be a melody. It is just such connections that form the basis of empathy.

Not everyone thinks that self-esteem is desirable. In fact, there are those who fear that promoting self-esteem will lead not to moral behavior but its opposite. There is a legitimate basis for this concern, and I share the concern to some extent. I have seen programs intended to promote self-esteem that are puerile and self-centered. After all, altruism, benevolence, kindness, and consideration require taking the interests and concerns of others to heart, whereas self-esteem, in its emphasis on the individual self, turns a blind eye to other people. Self-esteem is a part of the philosophy of individualism, which holds up the individual above everyone and everything else.

We can point to numerous examples of self-esteem and self-ishness going hand in hand. There are parents who want their children to feel good about themselves even if it is at the expense of others. Other people may be impediments to their goals. They value their own success or happiness above everything else. Cooperation, kindness, and consideration take a backseat to winning, getting, and getting more.

Parents (or schools) who promote their children's interests and emphasize self-esteem at others' expense rarely see what they are doing as immoral. They may even say that they are being responsible, doing what all parents are supposed to do—making sure their children succeed. Most of us cast a dim eye on such rationalizations. But even if we grant some measure of truth to the claim, it isn't social responsibility that these parents are after. The dreams for their children are not ethical, the values may not be moral values. A bigger house, a better job is what matters, not being an ethical person.

The hesitation about encouraging self-esteem rests on the fear that it leads to self-centeredness. If all that matters to me is meeting my own needs and desires, then others are there to be used for my own purposes. Bullies can feel good about themselves because others cower before them, and accomplished thieves can feel good about being successful at their work. Some who stress self-esteem are not interested in promoting morality but something quite different. Their ultimate aim is to raise confident and competent and successful children. In Jericho, Long Island, a girls' varsity basketball coach left her job with just six games left in the season. She was forced out, she said, because she refused to give the school board president's daughter more playing time. "He said that I was hurting his daughter, that I was using poor judgment as a coach." In an article in *Newsday*, the former coach said that the school board president had berated her for "destroying his daughter's self-esteem" by not allowing her to play more often.

Perhaps the girl's ego would have been boosted by more playing time; perhaps she was hurt by being benched. Clearly her parents stood behind her, supported her, and wanted her to succeed. But that has nothing to do with ethics or, you might say, the story illustrates the opposite of what many of us mean by ethical behavior. The story reminds me of a joke I once heard. "A customer comes into my store," the father says to his son. "He pays for the suit and leaves. After he's gone I notice that he gave me twenty dollars too much." Having reached the crux of the moral dilemma, he hesitates a moment, then asks his son, "So, what do I do? Tell my partner or not?"

The boy may be learning a lesson in taking control of his life and how to succeed in business, but the lesson is an immoral one. Perhaps the boy in the joke was the real-life Nick Leeson, the twenty-nine-year-old futures trader who caused the collapse of Barings Bank through unauthorized operations that resulted in $1.3 billion in losses. Although Leeson confessed to his crimes and served time in prison, he seems to take pride in his deeds. He writes that his bosses were stupid but he will be able to "face all my family and friends and look them in the eye." Although Leeson is a criminal, he hasn't lost face or pride or self-esteem, because what he prides himself on is cleverness, not moral behavior. He is a criminal, he admits. But, he thinks, that's nothing compared to others who are stupid—that, in Leeson's eyes, is despicable. You can't help but wonder how being smart became more important than being honest.

Professors of education Edward Wynne and Kevin Ryan examined self-esteem programs in schools throughout the country. They found that some schools that stressed self-esteem as a major educational objective actually "fostered a corrosive form of narcissism."

All this is true. But it is an error to think that self-centeredness necessarily flows from self-esteem or that it is possible to be moral with low self-esteem. Columbia University social scientist Elizabeth Midlarsky found that when people volunteered to help others, their feelings of self-esteem were augmented. Taking pride in what they had done didn't make them more selfish. Just the opposite. It made them more likely to volunteer to help others in the future.

There is an assumption that stands behind the criticism of self-esteem. The presupposition is that there is a fixed quantity of esteem to go around; and if I have more of it for myself, then there is less for you. But this isn't any more so for esteem than it is for love. Neither is a fixed quantity. I didn't love my wife less when my son was born and I didn't love my son less when my daughter was born. And when my grandchildren were born—well, I've never been so full of love in my life. Although I have a finite amount of time, even that isn't as fixed as I sometimes think. I thought I couldn't spare another moment until my granddaughter came along. I made time for her not by giving up anything but working more efficiently. I don't have to do that with love. Love simply expands. The same with self-esteem, under the right circumstances.

The real objection to self-esteem, then, isn't pride as such but an excessive concern with oneself to the exclusion of others. It is having too much self-regard that is the problem. If I am proud of who I am, that's fine. But if this means I believe that I am better than others, then something has gone wrong. And the reason not to boast or to flaunt one's talents or successes is that it breeds resentment or makes other people feel worse. Boasting is a type of competitiveness that undermines the self-esteem of those who come up short. Only one person, group, or team can be number one. Everyone else fails in relation to that. At the end of a championship game, we often see the defeated team sitting dejectedly, with tears in their eyes. They can't speak, as though being second best were no good at all. They are acting like they are failures because only being first is good enough. This is, of course, nonsense. It is playing the best one can and playing fairly that count, not that someone is better than you. Feeling proud of your family is a good thing but not when it means that you think that there is something wrong with other families; being proud of one's ethnic group or nation is fine, as long as it doesn't lead one to derogate other ethnic groups or countries. To believe that no one is better than you are isn't the same as believing that no one is as good as you are. It is crossing such boundaries that is the objection to self-esteem.

If we look at self-esteem through the Kohlberg theory of stages of moral reasoning, we see that the person who thinks well of himself but is at the same time egotistical is at the first stages of development. The implication for young children is that self-esteem may well be associated with being self-centered. But if the child is developing and being encouraged to identify with the feelings of others and to think critically, this is a phase, not a destination. Rather than trying to get the child to be less self-involved, it is more effective and helpful to speak about who you as an adult admire and why, to explain how you understand morality and why, and to support your child's inner life.

So while there is real reason to worry about instilling in children an attitude of self-love that is selfish, it is selfishness that bothers us, not self-esteem. I think the correct way to understand the warnings against pride is to rephrase the various injunctions this way: Never think less of yourself than you are; never think that you are more than another.

Aristotle understood that proper pride isn't a vice but a virtue. "Moral virtue," he explained, "is . . . a mean between two vices, one of excess and the other of deficiency, and . . . it aims at hitting the mean point in feelings and actions."

Courage

Proper pride is linked to another virtue: courage. Too much confidence leads to foolhardiness and too little courage leads to cowardice. "Cowards feel fear on inappropriate occasions or respond to fear and danger without confidence and self-control—that is, they are deficient in self-confidence or self-control," writes philosopher Mike Martin.

We all want our children to have self-confidence and competence—to have self-esteem—because we believe it leads to something greater. Self-esteem is a means toward an end. Proper pride and courage are values in the service of some other values. Philosophers refer to these types of values as "instrumental goods." The value serves as an instrument to achieve something that is good in itself, an "intrinsic good." Sometimes we are confused, not knowing if something is good because it helps us get something else or if it is good in and of itself. Money is an example. With no money at all we couldn't survive in a modern society. We pay the rent or mortgage, buy food, purchase clothes. I once visited a Christian commune for a week. Despite the Bruderhof's efforts to separate itself from modern society, it couldn't eliminate money totally. No matter how self-sufficient, the commune still needed to buy gasoline for its vehicles and pay its electric bills. But after we have secured the basic necessities, why do we need money? To buy other things that make life easier and sweeter. There are others, though, who want money for its own sake. Their satisfaction derives from having lots of it, and the more the better. Here money is both a means and an end—having it leads to happiness and happiness consists in having more of it.

Courage is a virtue because it allows us to act on our moral principles. Without courage we would frequently say one thing but do another. It wouldn't make us hypocrites exactly. We would believe what we said. We just couldn't do anything about it. We'd lack the ability to act. This is why we use the expression

"The courage of one's convictions." Without courage, convictions remain theoretical only. Some Germans deplored the Nazis but did nothing to stop them, because they were afraid. Some whites supported young Ruby Bridge's right to attend an integrated school, but kept silent because they were afraid of reprisals.

Citizens of Billings, Montana, a few years ago offered a stirring example of moral courage. Someone had thrown a rock through the window of a house that displayed a menorah. If Jews kept their menorahs publicly displayed they risked becoming future targets. Thousands of non-Jewish families responded by putting menorahs in the windows of their own homes.

Adding modern psychological insights to Aristotle's philosophy of virtue, we can say that because self-esteem is one of the components of confidence, confidence is needed to act courageously.

Self-esteem—confidence plus courage—is important because it helps us achieve the kind of life we desire. And if we desire to be moral, then self-esteem is necessary to be an ethical person.

11.

Treat Your Children with Respect

Respect your child and he will learn to respect himself; from you, he will understand the importance of treating other people as they should be treated.

This is the basis of religious and secular ethics: Love your neighbor as yourself. It is offered by nearly every religious and moral code. There are variations of this, such as: Do unto others as you would have them do unto you. Or its reverse: What is hateful to you, do not do to another. They all express the same basic idea.

The notion is that people must hold themselves in reasonably high regard to extend themselves to others. The rule is to treat another as you want them to treat you. If you thought you were an unworthy person, then you would, in turn, treat others as though they weren't worth anything either.

There is no question that parents and other adults need to be in charge of children, both in a legal and a moral sense. But there are ways to be both responsible and respectful. The key is to ask yourself how you would feel if your child treated you in the same way as you treat her. Are you polite to her? Do you allow her the freedoms appropriate for her age? When she asks you a question, do you give her thoughtful responses? Do you discipline her in such a way that leaves her sense of dignity intact?

Children are in constant need of correction. Who isn't? No one is perfect, ever. But remember the golden rule and apply it to how you treat your own child. Recall how *you* want(ed) to be treated and put yourself in your child's place. With that in mind, you will treat your child with respect.

If you want your children to respect you and others, then you have to show respect to them. If you don't, your words will be hypocritical and will fall on deaf ears.

This is one of my favorite stories about respecting children. It is told by Shmuel Auidor Hacohen.

Once there was a boy who thought he was a chicken. He had taken off all his clothes and sat naked under the family table. He scratched at the food fallen from the plates above. No matter what they tried, his parents couldn't convince him to return to the table.

So they called upon one of the wise people in the town. "Invite me for dinner one night," the teacher said. "I'll see what I can do."

The teacher sat down at the table. But just as the food was brought, he got up from his chair, took off his clothes and joined the boy under the table.

"What are you doing here?" he asked the boy.

"I'm a chicken," the boy replied with some surprise.

"That's some coincidence. So am I," the teacher said.

They sat together for a long time, the boy looking warily at the guest.

"Do you think a chicken can't wear a shirt?" the teacher asked the boy after a while. The boy shrugged. "Certainly a chicken can wear a shirt and still be a chicken."

The teacher signaled the parents to pass them shirts. The boy and the teacher then each put on a shirt.

"Do you think that just because someone is wearing pants he can't still be a chicken?" The boy looked at him. "Of course he can."

Two pairs of pants were passed below the table and they put them on.

It continued like this until they were both completely clothed.

Later the teacher said to the boy, "Do you think that because someone eats human food he can't be a chicken?" The boy smiled. "Of course he can."

So plates of food were passed to them and they both ate heartily.

Then the guest said, "Do you think a chicken has to sit under a table? It is possible for a chicken to sit at the table and still be himself."

The boy let out a laugh, and the two of them crawled out from under the table and sat in their chairs as a mound of ice cream and fruit was brought for dessert.

12.

Express Interest in Your Children's Activities, Projects, and Dreams

The single most important factor for your child's self-esteem is your involvement. I don't mean going to Jennifer's soccer games and cheerleading or trying to become Kevin's best friend. But it does mean letting your children know that you are interested in what they think and do. You need to make it clear that they matter to you and that you care about them.

Nothing is worse than being abandoned; perhaps second worse is being ignored. The first is a primal fear that reaches deep into our animal brains, and the second is linked to our need to be part of a human group. It isn't merely that children need guidance—they also need to feel wanted.

What circumstances make it more likely than not that a child will wind up as prosocial adult? The answer is being raised in a home where he feels wanted, where he feels secure, where he feels that he matters to others. Children from such homes have high self-esteem and believe that they can control events in their lives. They have a sense of personal responsibility for what happens to them.

So finding a place for a child in the family, making your child feel as though what he did interests you and matters to you are important building blocks of self-esteem.

When you take an interest in your child's activities, your son or daughter is getting a powerful message. You are saying, "You are important to me. I want to take care of you. What you do matters to me."

These are messages of concern, as well as protection. When

a child experiences the benevolent interest of an adult, she knows that the adult won't let her get lost or do something too dangerously stupid. And when a child already has the attention of an adult, he need not engage in outrageous (sometimes antisocial) behavior to get attention.

Parents who are demonstrably interested in the lives and activities of their children and provide warm, protective, stable, and nurturing homes have children with good self-images. The children have an inner security that allows them to act on their own consciences. With respect and solid emotional support, children usually are ready to accept themselves. Feeling emotionally secure, they don't feel threatened by rejection or even ridicule from their peers. They can accept differences among people, even when there is great pressure to conform when they are teenagers. Having been appreciated, they can appreciate others, even those who are not like themselves.

A positive self-image is also likely to breed empathy in your child. Feeling good about herself allows her to be open to the world around her. Accepting herself allows her to easily accept others. Self-esteem, competency, courage, and empathy are frequently found together. So your daughter can imagine what it is like to be another person. In other words, she is capable of identifying with the lives of those who may be very different from her.

So get involved, find out (if you don't already know) what your child is doing, ask questions about what he thinks. But don't go too far. There is a line that can be crossed between interest and overinvolvement. Support and encourage your child, but don't smother him. Don't do for him what he can do for himself and give him room to learn from his mistakes.

Somewhere between being thrown into a pool to sink or swim and never being allowed into the pool without water wings, there is the right balance.

Here is a passage from Kahlil Gibran's *The Prophet* that expresses these sentiments beautifully:

Your children are not your children.
They are the sons and daughters of Life's longing for
itself.
They come through you but not from you,
And though they are with you yet they belong not to
you.
You may give them your love but not your thoughts,
For they have their own thoughts.
You may house their bodies but not their souls,
For their souls dwell in the house of tomorrow, which
you cannot visit, not even in your dreams.
You may strive to be like them, but seek not to make
them like you.
For life goes not backward nor tarries with yesterday.
You are the bows from which your children as living
arrows are sent forth.
The archer sees the mark upon the path of the infinite,
and He bends you with His might that His arrows
may go swift and far.
Let your bending in the archer's hand be for gladness;
For even as He loves the arrow that flies, so He loves
also the bow that is stable.

13.

Help Set Goals and Encourage Your Children to See Them Through

Spell out what you want from your children and why. If you are clear about both goals and limits, you will likely have children with high self-esteem. Your expectations, however, must be both realistic and slightly out of reach.

Mastering a skill, little by little, leads to the belief that it is possible to control events in one's life. Just think of the joy that crossed your child's face when she learned how to read. She learned how to crack the word code letter by letter, sound by sound, book by book.

What does this have to do with raising ethical children? Remember, self-esteem and self-efficacy are underpinnings of moral behavior—the belief that it is possible to be responsible because what you do makes a difference.

Our expectations can hurt our children when what we want from them is unrealistic. Persistent failure doesn't produce confidence but its opposite. If you expect Kevin to be a dancer when he trips over his own feet, he eventually gives up, knowing that no matter what he does, his efforts are doomed. If Jennifer can't master a simple tune on the piano because she is tone deaf, she suffers the humiliation of disappointing her parents again and again.

Holding out realistic goals appropriate for a child's age and encouraging him to see them through is yet another way of telling your child that we care about him, that we understand him.

Self-esteem is enhanced by competence, because it leads to control over the environment. A person who is competent is, at least in some measure, in control of her own life.

14.

Praise a Task Well Done

Your children want to please you. So let them know when they succeed. Praise them for what they have done well; a repeat performance won't be far behind.

Most parents know this. But some take this to mean that they shouldn't be critical of their children at all. Wanting to boost their child's ego, they will praise everything he does. They do everything they can to shield their son from criticism, refusing to tell him he has done something wrong or less than perfect.

So Kevin comes home with a drawing, and it goes on the refrigerator; Jennifer writes a poem, and it gets framed and hung on the wall. You believe that you can boost your children's self-esteem by being cheerleaders. "Great, Kevin!" we gush, even though the drawing shows no effort. "Terrific, Jennifer!" we say, even though the poem is a knock-off of yesterday's birthday card. Every effort is praised to the skies, even if the effort is, by any object standard, mediocre or worse.

Parents (and teachers) shouldn't be cheerleaders. Think of yourself as a good coach. She doesn't yell, "You jerk," if Jennifer doesn't kick the ball right. But she also doesn't say, "Excellent job," when the performance was a poor one. Jennifer can be praised for having made a great effort, if that is what she did; but if she didn't play a great game, telling her she did only builds false confidence.

Cheerleaders have a job to do, too, rushing onto the field and singing the team's praises even if the team really is a dud. It's part of their job description. They are there to boost the team's and players' spirits. Their team is always the greatest team, even if it trails the league in everything.

The coach, on the other hand, points out strengths—good effort, fine try—but also weaknesses. "That was good," a coach might say. "But don't be distracted by your friends in the stands. You need to keep you eye on the ball. Now let's try it again."

Self-esteem rests on a realistic picture of oneself. Boosterism presents a false picture of accomplishments. Eventually, a child will see through the cheerleading, if that's all there is. Far better to present the truth with kindness than falsehoods that create self-deception.

Criticism should be presented with respect.

All children do some things well. Focus on what those strengths are and build on them. At the same time, let your child know that there are matters that need improvement and that there is a goal she hasn't yet reached. Achieving it will require persevering in spite of frustrations. Learning to deal with frustration is essential for moral character—especially when doing the right thing isn't easy.

There is a balance to be found between total acceptance and constant criticism. This kind of balance means that your child will be respected for who he truly is. To be known this way is critical, for it says to your child—you are a real person, not a model or an image or some hoped-for unrealized child.

15.

Give Your Children Emotional and Verbal Support to Stand Against the Crowd When Necessary

Tell Jennifer that you are proud of her for standing up for what she believes, even if it makes her unpopular. Give her all the emotional support she needs when she finds herself scorned by others. Jennifer needs you to help her do the right thing when the pressure is on to do the opposite. It's sometimes difficult to act morally. Pressure to conform is powerful, and so is the desire to fit in.

But there are times when being good and doing right require courage. It isn't enough to know what to do or even to want to do the right thing. We also need the strength to do it.

When the most popular girls in school pick on Jennifer's best friend, she may know what is right and may want to do it, but she may have trouble taking action. She may even tell you that she wants to leave her friend to go along with everyone else. But deep down, she really wants your guidance and unconsciously longs for it. That's why she came to you in the first place. She needs your help, because she isn't quite strong enough alone.

Moral courage is different than daredevil risk taking. Moral courage doesn't require physical strength but inner fortitude. That strong fiber is also related to self-esteem. Moral courage is the ability to stand against the crowd when necessary.

Those who simply go along with the crowd are seldom ethical people in the fullest sense of that word. In many respects, they may be decent and moral. Followers may not lie—as long as everyone else tells the truth. They may not cheat—as long as everyone else is honest. But they *will* lie if the crowd they hang out with are liars, and they *will* cheat if their crowd is dishonest.

Behaving morally means acting as a worthy and competent person. This, in turn, is influenced by the level and quality of our self-esteem.

Whatever else you do, let Jennifer know how proud you are that she has the courage of her convictions.

Discipline

Behavior Has Consequences

Don't make a fence that is more important than what is fenced in.

—THE MIDRASH, Genesis Rabbah

Your children need to be disciplined at one time or another. And you may be tempted to use the three traditional methods of fear, guilt, and shame. But will these shape a child into a moral adult? Probably not. Something different is needed when our goal is raising a moral child. Children disciplined with fear become too fearful to act courageously when they need to; children raised with guilt are too consumed with their own feelings to care about another's; and a child raised with shame doesn't have the confidence to do the right thing when the going gets tough.

Fear, guilt, and shame are an unnecessary part of the disciplinary diet. Responsible, mature, moral behavior has nothing to do with the traditional methods of raising moral children.

So what is the best way for you to discipline your child? The answer is pretty clear. Laurence Steinberg of Temple University reports that since the late 1950s "literally hundreds of studies have been conducted that examine acceptance, firmness, and autonomy support and their consequences for the child's development. The gist of these studies has been remarkably consistent." Steinberg finds that children develop into responsible adults when their parents are accepting and firm but not stern. They also support the child's developing sense of being an independent person. These parents steer a course between being permissive and being authoritarian. Some researchers have termed them "authoritative" parents.

The discipline that seems to be most effective for raising a moral child involves an explanation of other's feelings, for example, "Sharing makes other children happy." Such a statement is more likely to be accepted and internalized by the child than a statement that appears to be a reason but really isn't, such as "It's good to share." Your children are more likely to accept the values you're trying to teach them when you take your children aside and firmly state your expectations of them.

It is important to note one of the findings of Fogelman's research on rescuers of Jews in Germany. She writes, "The essential characteristic of moral individuals is . . . their conscience can transcend an evil society because that conscience is independent and has its origins in early childhood." Rescuers took action because they could think independently of the crowd around them. Some knew their hearts spoke the truth and ignored Nazi propaganda. Others believed strongly enough in moral principles to lead them to dismiss the messages of hatred that surrounded them.

For two thousand years, Aesop's fables have taught moral lessons. Some of the stories offer sound advice and helpful moral insights, for example, "Androcles and the Lion." It is the story of a slave boy who removes a thorn from a lion's paw. One day the boy and the lion were sent to the circus. The boy was put in the arena and the lion, let loose. As soon as the lion recognized the boy, instead of tearing him to pieces, he fawned upon him. Androcles explained the story to the emperor, whereupon the slave was pardoned and the lion, set loose to return to the forest. The story ends with an aphorism about gratitude.

Unfortunately, many of the stories use fear or punishment as a teaching technique. They often end with warnings, such as "Beware of insincere friends" and "Don't bite the hand that feeds you." In fact, most of the fables define morality in terms of Kohlberg's stage 1 or stage 2 thinking. Although young children can readily understand the point of the story, the problem is that it reinforces their present level rather than stimulating them to think at a higher level. In fact, children learn best when presented with material that is geared to a slightly higher development level.

This is not to say that fear should play no role in moral behavior. Frightening your child just before she is going to stick a finger into an electric outlet may be your only choice at the time. But emergencies are the exception. If you rely on fear as a teaching tool, you are not preparing your children adequately for a complex world full of difficult choices.

Most everything I've written about in this book so far has taken a positive slant. This isn't the traditional way. Just as many parents still believe that to spare the rod is to spoil the child, there are many who believe that guilt and shame should also be used as a childrearing technique. Because guilt and shame have been so widely used to get children to do the right thing, I want to spend most of this section talking about the role of guilt in raising your child. This may seem a bit negative—more of what *not* to do than what *to* do—but I include it because these two emotions are so powerful that we can easily lapse into using them as a way of getting our children to do the right thing. What's more, inducing guilt and shame has been used by so many for so long, it would be unfair to simply dismiss these emotions without looking at them in some detail. It's not possible to talk about raising a moral child without spending some time on the negative.

Guilt

Guilty feelings arise when we have violated a moral norm that we accept as valid. If your child steals money from you purse, for example, she will feel guilty if she both knows that stealing is wrong and accepts the rule is a correct one. A person who feels guilty, notes philosopher Herbert Morris, is "one who has internalized norms and, as such, is committed to avoiding wrong." A definition of a *psychopath* is someone who hasn't accepted society's basic moral rules and, therefore, doesn't feel guilty when he does something immoral. On the other hand, many reformers deliberately brake social conventions to create a more ethical society. They also don't feel guilty for what they have done. Quite the opposite: They would have felt guilty if they had continued to live in an unjust world without trying to change it.

An interesting aspect of feeling guilty is that many people feel guilty when they hurt another person even if it was unintentional or unavoidable. Psychologists Nico Frijda and Batja Mesquita of the University of Amsterdam find that nearly half the people they interviewed felt guilty for having caused unintended harm, such as hurting one's mother when leaving home to marry. So as your child reaches adolescence he may be torn between loyalty to you and loyalty to his friends. And he may well feel guilty without being able to resolve the dilemma. It does no good to talk him out of feeling guilty. The feeling is a natural consequence of his moral sense.

A person may also feel guilty about having hurt someone accidentally. Carelessness is as much a source of guilt as intentional harm. For example, if your child hurt someone with a foul ball, she may suffer from guilt feelings. You can assure her that it was only an accident, but there is nothing wrong with the feelings she has. Again, she has them because she is a responsible person and guilt is one of the burdens of being ethical.

Guilt is useful in so far as it makes us more cautious or moves us to socially responsible action. The sociopath never experiences such feelings and, therefore, poses a danger to society; the neurotic experiences so much of it that he can't function normally.

People who think of themselves as victims do so because

they believe they have no control over their lives. They don't feel responsible and, therefore, don't feel guilty either. A student once told me that he wouldn't be in class the following day because was going to court to defend himself against a speeding ticket he had received. I asked if he had really broken the speed limit. "Yes," he said, "but it wasn't my fault." I wondered how that could be. He smiled and said, "Other people were going faster than I was. I was only trying to keep up." Did he really believe this, I wondered? As far as I could tell, he didn't feel the least bit guilty for having broken the law. If he saw the incident as trivial, that would be one thing. Then, with some education, he could see how speeding endangers not only himself but others. But if he was sincere in blaming his speeding on others, I wondered what other of his failures he blamed others for. It was the classic excuse "everyone else does it" of the cheat, the liar, and the thief.

So, then, if guilt follows from being moral, why shouldn't we use it to raise a moral child? The clear conclusion from the studies on guilt is that using guilt as a tool to *establish* moral standards is bound to fail. Guilt—healthy guilt—flows from morality, not the other way around. If people feel guilty when they have done wrong, it is because they already possess a moral compass. But if they are lacking the rudiments of moral feelings, then deliberately instilling guilt won't create an ethical person. It will more likely create an angry, hostile person.

Shame

Shame, too, is related to morality. When people fail to meet moral standards, they feel ashamed.

When I was a teenager, a boy my age and his family moved into my apartment building. I took an instant dislike to him. To this day, I can't tell you why. He had never done anything to me. I hardly knew him and don't remember speaking to him. Yet I picked on him mercilessly, giving him an ugly nickname and bad-mouthing him to others. Finally his mother spoke to mine about what I was doing. I had been caught and now felt awful. How could I do such a thing? What was going on with me? I'm not sure, but I knew that I was ashamed. I had let a lot of people down.

If I hadn't been caught, I may not have felt ashamed at all. Perhaps I would have outgrown whatever was propelling me and then forgotten about it. But to this day I reflect on my behavior of one of the shameful episodes in my life. We don't always have to be caught to feel ashamed of ourselves. When a girl, my wife took change from her parents' savings jar. When her mother suspected the cleaning lady, Lyn kept her mouth shut. Her parents never did find out that Lyn took the money, but my wife hasn't forgotten the incident and still feels ashamed of her behavior. No one needed to know that she took the money for her to feel ashamed.

I felt terrible for what I did because I cared what my parents thought of me. If I hadn't cared about what others thought of me or cared about living up to my own standards, I wouldn't have felt ashamed. "If all respect for the self is lost, the knowledge that the self has betrayed a friend [for example] will not arouse shame," psychologist Carl Schneider writes. "The person may experience self-contempt, or numbness, but shame implies that the person *cares*."

Shame is a painful experience because we have been emotionally separated from other people. Of the two—guilt and shame—psychoanalyst Helen Block Lewis believes that shame is by far the more painful. The suicide rates in America and Japan seem to bear this out. Anthropologists characterize Japan as a culture of shame. When a person has done something wrong, he frequently experiences it as a personal failure. Although there are few people in prisons in Japan, the suicide rate is much higher than that in the United States. Young people are ashamed for

letting down their parents and teachers by not excelling scho-
lastically; fired workers are ashamed for having let down their
families.

Block believes that shame is so painful because we perceive
shame as a deficiency within ourselves. Whereas guilt is always
related to a moral transgression, disappointment or defeat may
lead to shame. "Shame," Block writes, "is about the *self*, while
guilt is about *something*." Shame gets right to the sense of who
we are and what kind of people we are. The self is the focal
point of shame, but the focal point of guilt is the action taken.
Poet Robert Hass writes, "The core of the self, we learn early,
is where shame lives."

Today it seems people are all too willing to broadcast the
most personal, intimate details of their lives. Some conservatives, such as William Bennett, Gertrude Himmelfarb, and William Buckley, feel we have gone too far in playing down both
guilt and shame. What is missing in America today, these critics
claim, is shame and the lack of shame is the cause of America's
moral crisis. Their point is that incivility and lack of self-
restraint, which are exhibited daily on television talk shows, for
example, indicate the decline and ultimate demise of civilization
as we know it. Many political and religious conservatives point
to out-of-wedlock births, soaring prison populations, abortions
on demand, and high divorce rates as signals of an immoral
society. Social workers, therapists, and liberal judges have taken
the brunt of criticism for doing away with guilt and shame. For
example, the Menendez brothers, who murdered their parents,
were found not guilty in their first trial, because they were por-
trayed as victims of child abuse. They weren't responsible for
their actions, because their father had beaten them. So instead
of being judged as wicked and, therefore, guilty, some jurors
defined them as people incapable of acting responsibly. They
couldn't be held accountable for their actions. They were to be
pitied, not scorned. They need treatment, those jurors believed,
not jail time.

Has morality been replaced by psychobabble? Is no one responsible for the bad things they do? No more coddling! these folks say.

Why, then, have guilt and shame fallen into disuse? And why would anyone object to restoring them to their former place?

The answers to these two questions are intimately related. There are good reasons why guilt and shame have fallen out of disfavor with many parents and educators. History is filled with the wreckage of those who grew up under clouds of guilt and shame. Freud understood that neurotic guilt caused a great deal of psychological and physical misery. Guilt and shame broke people's spirits as surely as binding broke the feet of Chinese women. People suffocated when forced to conform to stultifying standards. Although many people left small towns for better jobs, just as many left to get away from prying eyes of neighbors. Consequently, much of the intellectual and social history of the late nineteenth and the twentieth centuries follows revolts against the stifling atmosphere in which families and societies frowned on individual expression.

Shame atrophied as an acceptable method of discipline as Western philosophy raised respect for the person to center stage. Individual worth replaced social status as the central moral consideration. Once respect for the individual permeated the thinking of the general public, societal and family norms fell to the side, replaced by the value of the dignity of the individual. This wasn't the only reason for the decline of strong social control by the group but one of several forces. In the United States, development of the modern economy and the restlessness that accompanied settlement of the west and immigration from Europe facilitated this change. While continuing to value community on the one hand, America came to understand the oppressive aspects of defining oneself strictly through a group. On the other hand, Americans preferred making their own identities to accepting an inherited one or one thrust on them by others. Throughout the twentieth century, conformity was defined in negative terms, especially in America, where liberty was taken as a primary value.

As a result of these societal changes, shame as a method of social control fell into disuse. A number of years ago, I met someone who found himself in the middle of this tug between community pressure and individual desire. I was visiting a religious commune in the central plains of Montana when one of the young Huterite cowboys asked if I would like to ride with him. We mounted a pair of horses and galloped to the far side of the barn. We sat atop our stallions, and he leaned over to talk to me softly. He couldn't talk to any of his friends on the commune, and he certainly couldn't talk to his family. They wouldn't understand. Besides, he was also feeling ashamed for what he was thinking. He asked for a cigarette, a forbidden indulgence on the ranch. He then proceeded to tell me about his dreams and how he one day planned to leave Star Colony. He respected his parents, he said, but he disliked living there. Everyone told him what to think, what to do, what to wear, what to eat. So many rules governed his life that he felt as though he couldn't be himself. He wanted to be free, but he also liked the extended family and the community he had known all his life.

I don't know what he decided to do. I can understand his conflicting feelings. Group pressure can be suffocating; but at the same time, it is lonely without a community. There is as much a need and a desire to belong as there is a pull to be our own person.

Shame works, if what we want is for people to conform. People do act on the moral norms of their society as a result of being shamed. But the virtues attained this way aren't very strong. It's like a lake frozen over by a thin sheet of ice. The surface looks inviting to skaters, but it really isn't strong enough to hold their weight. Those who are motivated by fear, guilt, or shame are far more likely to be the bystanders rather than the rescuers, as in Nazi Europe. Unable to think critically, they are incapable of overcoming the limitations of their own society. Many Germans, after all, were good people. Fathers took care of their families, mothers cooked for their children. Shame, which aims at social cohesion, produces conformity in thinking and, therefore, fails as a method of moral education.

So although the calls for shame have an element of appeal and, in certain narrow instances may be desirable, such invitations should also raise a red flag of caution. The element of shame that some find so attractive is also troubling, namely, that shame is designed to lower a person's self-esteem. The conservatives are right: shame and lowered self-esteem do go together. The more you make someone ashamed, the lower will be her self-esteem. Shame is effective precisely because it gets to the very heart of how a person judges herself or feels about herself. Shaming a person may destroy what little self-respect a person possesses, leading to more hostility, not prosocial behavior. It is more likely to create a bystander than a rescuer. The extensive personality isn't built on shame. Rather the moral person feels shame when she has acted shamefully.

Here is a story from India:

Once a teacher summoned a group of students. "Our temple is nearly in ruins," he said. "The paint is flaking from the walls, the steps are too dangerous to walk upon. We are very poor, so I have devised a plan."

The students waited eagerly to hear the teacher's words of wisdom.

"Each of you will go into town and steal something of value. You will bring it back and we'll sell it. With the money we will rebuild our temple and school. But you must be very careful. Make sure no one sees you."

The students were amazed that their teacher could make such a suggestion.

When the teacher left, they discussed the plan amongst themselves.

"It is wrong to steal," one suggested.

Everyone agreed.

"But the teacher wouldn't tell us to do something immoral. So there must be a good reason."

"Yes," another one said. "If our school were beautiful, we would attract students. Then more people would be educated and everyone would know right from wrong."

They continued the discussion a bit longer, then went to town. All except one student, who stood alone in the courtyard.

The teacher saw him and asked, "Why didn't you go with the others?"

"It is wrong to steal," he said.

"But no one would see you."

"I will see myself with my own eyes," the student said.

"I was just testing my students," the teacher said. "You are the only one who has passed."

With that he embraced the student.

16.

Be Flexible—Not Arbitrary—in Your Discipline

Be consistent but flexible when disciplining your child. Be firm but not rigid. It is important that he knows what to expect from you. Kevin needs to know what the family rules are and what happens when they are broken. He also needs to know that he will be held accountable for his transgressions.

This isn't to say that there aren't exceptions to rules. Of course there are. Everyone recognizes extenuating circumstances. We offer understanding and support. But understanding is not the same as excusing.

Establishing rules for your children's behavior lets them know what they can and cannot do, what we expect of them. This indirectly expresses to our children what we value. But if we don't consistently apply our rules, then we may as well not have them at all. If you are arbitrary in disciplining your children, the lesson they learn is that they can't really count on you. One day they sneak an extra cookie at dinner and they're indulged, another time punished. One time they are ignored, another time reprimanded.

Another unwanted lesson learned by arbitrary discipline is that rules don't really mean anything. Rather than being tied to something sensible and understandable, children begin to see the rules as capricious, whims of the person wielding the power.

There's no question that all children need to be disciplined at one time or another. Naturally curious, children push to the limits. They want to run into the surf, poke their fingers into holes, and get their hands on their older brother's videos. They are also selfish and self-centered at times. Your responsibility as an adult is to provide them with limits to protect their well-being and to teach them how to be better people.

It's not unusual to see children being cruel to others. Kevin's frustration gets out of hand, and he gets into a fight. Jennifer lashes out at her friend, hitting her when she reaches for Jennifer's favorite doll. Far more important than punishment is helping them to see the harm they have caused and showing them how to make amends. I don't mean a verbal apology, although sometimes that is helpful. "Tell Kevin that you are sorry you took away his book," doesn't really get to the bottom of the matter. An apology is important, but more important is for both Jennifer and Kevin to know that Jennifer broke the rules and hurt another. You can say, "Taking is wrong, Jennifer. Look how upset your brother is now. What do you think you can do to make him happy?" Suggest ways to remedy the hurt they have done. "Do you think that maybe I can read the story to both of you now?" This is essential in keeping human relations in good repair.

Ideally, discipline comes from within. Self-control is more effective than restraints from outside. But inward discipline takes time to develop. Until then, you, the parent, must take charge by setting boundaries and helping your children understand them.

17.

Don't Use Intimidation; Never Use Ridicule

As Jennifer is about to punch Kevin, you shout at her, and she bursts into tears. You've frightened her out of doing the wrong thing. There was no time to reason with her; and besides, no matter what she might have said, you weren't going to let her hurt Kevin.

So intimidation does occasionally come in handy. It's the most direct route to cautious behavior. What's more, we can't always learn by doing, because we could kill ourselves before we learned the proper lesson.

But, as a rule, avoid intimidating children into good behavior. Fear gets stuck in a lower order of moral reasoning. Rather than encouraging Jennifer to understand the reasons behind the rules, intimidation simply reinforces stage 1 thinking: Do it because someone stronger has told you to and that is the reason it is right. Take away the fear of being caught and punished and what remains is the thrill of doing something forbidden and dangerous. This is one of the reasons many children who get into trouble because of doing something foolish come from homes where physical punishment and intimidation are means of discipline.

If the only reason Kevin behaves is because of fear of being punished, then there is no generalizing from one situation to another. He doesn't say, "This situation is like one before it, so I shouldn't do this here either." Remove the threat of being punished and everything is okay. If Kevin doesn't understand the reasons for moral behavior, he may be well behaved but get into trouble at the amusement park with his friends. He doesn't see that the same reasons apply in different situations.

As a parent, it's easy to rely on intimidation. We are bigger and stronger than our kids, so it is simple to loom over them, yelling with our big voices at them to do what we want.

Ridicule and sarcasm have their own problems as a discipline tool. Derision only makes children feel awful about themselves. When we say something like "How could you be so stupid?" they come to view themselves unworthy, incompetent, and irresponsible—precisely the opposite of the kind of feelings we want them to have.

Although there are occasionally good reasons to use intimidation ("Don't run into the street!"), there is never a good reason to mock children. Nevertheless, we all speak to our children this way at one time or another. We are under stress. We've had a long and stressful day and lose our heads. Then take the next opportunity to apologize to Kevin. We all make mistakes, parents included. Children should understand this. We often tell our children that apologizing is part of making up, and we should practice this once in a while on them. This is an important lesson to learn, and they can learn it from us, not through a lecture on good manners but by example.

When your child needs disciplining, calmly correct mistakes with firm guidance. "Don't do that again, Kevin. Sharing is important. It makes Jennifer feel bad when you do that. Please let her play with you." Not only does this avoid making the child feel foolish and shattering a fragile ego, it will show him the way he should be relating to others. You should treat your children the way you want them to treat others.

Frightened people often lack the courage to do good; children who are humiliated often become passive adults, ready to conform. Instead of meeting unfairness and abuse with moral indignation, they remain silent in the face of injustice.

There is an ancient Buddhist story that makes the point this way:

Long ago in India a black bull was born. The calf was so perfect in every way that the farmer called him Beauty.

The farmer treated the bull as though it were a precious child of his. He fed it the best food and he always treated it with great kindness. As time went on, not only did the calf grow even more beautiful, it also grew in strength until it was the strongest animal in the kingdom.

One day Beauty said to himself, "My master has treated me so kindly that I want to repay him in some way."

So Beauty proposed to the farmer that there be a contest to see which bull could pull the heaviest load. Beauty had no doubt that he could win and urged the farmer to wager a large sum, half of all he owned.

All the wealthy farmers gathered in the field with their bulls. Each in turn hitched their animals to a wagon and the wagon was loaded with stones. When Beauty's turn came, the farmer jumped on his back, whipped his side with a stick and shouted into his ear, "Pull you demon! You stupid bull! Pull!"

Beauty stood still, not moving a muscle, not pulling the loaded cart even one inch.

The farmer lost a large fortune that afternoon. When they returned home, the farmer sat with his head in his hands and cried.

"What can I do now? I'm now a poor man!"

Beauty stood beside his master and asked, "Have I ever harmed you?"

"Never," the farmer answered.

"Have I ever hurt your children?"

"No," said his master.

"Then tell me, why were you so cruel to me? Was it the thought of making so much money causing you to forget the respect you used to show me, your friend and servant?"

The farmer couldn't say a word.

"Now, if you arrange another contest, I'll help you

recover your money. This time wager the rest of the farm. But remember, you must treat me kindly."

This time at the contest the farmer stroked Beauty's sides, he patted his head and he talked to him softly and with great kindness. "Beauty, my bull. Show me your strength."

Beauty pulled more rocks that day than any other bull and the farmer recovered all that he had lost.

18.

The Severity of the Punishment Should Be Related to the Severity of the Wrongdoing

The idea that the punishment should fit the crime may seem obvious, but it isn't, at least not to children. Their notion of what it means to do wrong is different from ours. In the minds of young children, there are no accidents.

Children move from considering only the external and tangible results to paying attention to the motives underlying the action. Remember the conversation Swiss psychologist Jean Piaget had with five-year-old Constance. He said, suppose a girl were carrying a tray with five cups and she tripped and fell, breaking all the cups. Then suppose there was another girl who was angry, so she went to the cupboard and threw one cup to the floor and broke it. Which child did the worse thing?

The first one, Constance answered. Why? Because she broke five cups but the other girl broke only one. Breaking five is worse than breaking one.

Children, generally until about age five or so, don't distinguish between mishaps and intentions. They look only at the outcome. They haven't yet internalized an understanding of what stands behind moral rules. Children can see only the results, not the process or motivation.

This is why being fair for children means being equal. So if Jennifer stays up late, Kevin will insist on also being allowed to stay up late even though he is three years younger.

Children don't distinguish between equality and equity. But adults know the difference. The punishment we mete out to Jennifer should be age appropriate and reflect both her intentions and the seriousness of what she has done. Although Jennifer may not understand these distinctions and complain that you let Kevin get away with doing the same thing she has done, discipline, which is fair, does consider all the factors involved.

Making the punishment fit the crime, so to speak, is also another form of consistency. Children will come to learn that some transgressions are worse than others (and conversely, some good deeds are better than others). Calibrating the severity of the punishment to fit the wrongdoing lets your children know that there is a scale of values. We reward the things that are important and we punish the actions that are wrong. By punishing fairly, we are teaching about moral judgments.

So try not to make too much of small wrongdoings or make too little of the truly bad things. If Jennifer breaks a toy because she's angry, the punishment should be different from the one given if she hits her friend.

19.

Discipline with Explanations

Kevin needs to know why he is being disciplined. He may not agree with you or your reason; children seldom do. They cry, "That's no fair!" Who doesn't want to avoid being caught?

The point isn't to get him to agree with you but to get him to change his behavior. Of course, you can keep Kevin from absconding with another cookie if you threaten him enough. But, as mentioned earlier, this isn't an adequate form of discipline, if you're interested in raising a moral child, not merely a compliant one.

"Kevin, you know that you have to ask before taking a cookie," you can say. "None of us can just take what we want."

"But I wanted the cookie."

"But it's a treat. And when you want a treat, you have to ask first."

The discussion may stop there or Kevin may continue to press you for more adequate explanations. If you think back on the stages of moral reasoning, you can figure out a reason that is age appropriate. Remember, try to offer reasons that are just a bit ahead of your child's stage. This helps her to grasp the next level.

An explanation for the punishment is at least as important as the punishment itself. By offering this, your child understands that you have good reason to disapprove of what he has done. Although he will not fully grasp your explanation, Kevin will know that the strictures you put on him make sense. As he matures, he will grasp this more completely. Until then, he is assured that there is order in the world and that he lives within a structure that he can count on. He may not have the key to understanding yet, but he knows that he will acquire it in good time.

The parents of the people who became rescuers of Jews in Nazi Germany used this approach to discipline. Many of these parents used physical punishment, although sparingly, whereas others did not use it at all. What they had in common, though, was this: When their child harmed another, they suggested to their children ways to remedy the hurt they had done. They made great use of persuasion and advice.

These parents relied on reason, assuming that their children were intelligent. They believed that, at some level, their children could understand what they were after. To make the opposite assumption—children don't understand, so don't deserve an explanation—is to create a self-fulfilling prophecy.

If no explanations are given, Jennifer and Kevin have no reason to think that their being punished is anything other than their parents' vagaries. The message they will learn is that people can't be trusted and that you can't count on what they are going to do. They will not have developed self-discipline or a moral compass.

20.

Criticize in Private

No one enjoys being made to feel foolish. But we make children feel foolish all the time. We don't mean to. It's just that Jennifer is so cute and says the most adorable things. We can't help but laugh when she is this way. We are charmed. We talk about her to friends as though she weren't there and listening.

The trouble is that there are times when Jennifer doesn't *mean* to be funny. She is quite serious about what she is doing or saying. She uses the wrong word or she misunderstands a situation or her explanation is so delightful that we can't help but smiling and letting out a laugh. But if Jennifer were in earnest, she can feel only diminished. The next time she will be less forthcoming.

I often tell stories to children in the presence of their parents and other adults. At the end, I ask the children a question, but before I do I caution the adults to take the children seriously and to refrain from laughing. As adults, they know the laugh is friendly; children often don't understand that.

When your child says something seriously, respond in the same way. The guideline is no different than it is for most situations: Treat others as you want to be treated. Each of us can remember feeling foolish, and we know it is uncomfortable. It only weakens our self-esteem and makes us question our abilities.

The same with criticism. Of course Kevin needs correction when he rides his bike without permission, and constructive criticism is important. But do it in private. Criticizing in public leads to feeling humiliated. The lesson you teach this way may not be the lesson you want to teach. You want to change behavior, not shred a healthy ego.

There are times when you'll laugh at your daughter when

she means to be taken seriously and occasionally you'll criticize your son in public. We all lapse, we all make mistakes. The important thing is that you don't make it a regular practice and that you apologize sincerely when you do.

Curt's father's reaction to his athletic ineptitude is a good example of how to handle parental disappointment. Curt grew up the youngest of three boys in rural south Texas. His family, along with many other Texans, placed a high premium on sports. Both of Curt's older brothers made the family proud with their athletic prowess, playing on varsity teams—one in football and the other in track and field—from elementary school through college, no small achievement.

Curt's family expected him to follow his brothers' examples and wanted him to play baseball. However, Curt didn't have much interest in any sport. He played, nevertheless, not wanting to disappoint his parents. He picked up a baseball glove and joined Little League, but mostly he sat on the bench. But one day when his father was at the game and his team was far ahead, the coach put Curt in the outfield.

Years later Curt recalls that afternoon. He couldn't do anything right—hit, catch, or throw. He let balls sail over his head, and he dropped a pop fly that should have been routine. To this day he remembers the humiliation he felt—his failure as a player, the embarrassment at disappointing his family.

After the game he sat alone, holding his head in his hands, not wanting to look at anyone. His father walked over to him when everyone else had left. The two said nothing for a while, but Curt could feel tears flooding his eyes. His father put his arm on Curt's shoulder and asked, "You don't like baseball, do you?"

Curt told him he didn't like sports, that he wasn't any good as an athlete, and he didn't want to play any game ever again.

"That's all right, son," his father said. "You don't have to be an athlete. Someday you will discover what you do love. Now let's go home. Someday you'll find what your real talent is."

Habits

Morality Is Learned Through Observation and Doing

> The virtues arise in us neither by nature nor against nature but we are by nature able to acquire them and reach our complete perfection through habit.
> —ARISTOTLE, in *Nichomachean Ethics*

I'm preparing breakfast for my grandchildren. I rotate the oatmeal carton to read the nutrition facts. On the opposing panel I learn how I can prepare the cereal in a bowl or in the microwave. And on the back I see a mother feeding her toddler. I read the copy: "Developing Lifelong Tastes. Teaching your baby to eat a variety of healthy foods now can help establish healthy eating habits for a lifetime."

If only that were true. My wife and I gave our children healthy foods when they were that age. Oatmeal and dry cereal without sugar, orange juice and vegetables, meat and potatoes, little dessert, mainly fruit. We had no candy in the house. The first time my son was given a lollipop—he was about two—he took it by the cellophane and sucked on the stick.

But the allure of junk food was overwhelming. We may have even inadvertently contributed to it. Lyn liked baking, and she made many cakes and brownies. This seemed all right to us because they were homemade, not store bought. Using brown sugar and honey seemed a healthier choice than refined sugar. However, Eric's and Kori's tastebuds didn't make such distinctions. Our children now tell us that they used to stand guard until they saw our car disappear down the street. Once the coast was clear they would run to the grocery store, a few blocks away, to stock up on God knows what. Actually, we do know what because one day, while looking for misplaced clothing in our daughter's dresser, my wife found a stash of candy wrappers. Our children had figured out how to save money for the candy. What they couldn't figure out was how to get rid of the incriminating evidence.

Despite our valiant efforts to instill healthy eating habits in them, my son still pushes broccoli to the side and could live on sweet desserts, and my daughter is a happy consumer of soda and potato chips. They do try. My daughter bought baby food without preservatives for her daughter. And my son occasionally eats his salad—when his wife cajoles sufficiently. So maybe somehow the message resides deep in the recesses of their minds: Eat right. Maybe my wife and I haven't failed. We just need to wait longer.

We hope. And so it is we hope that the moral guidance we offered throughout their childhood with our words and deeds will also make a difference in the long run. We assume that acting morally as an adult will come naturally to those who have been raised on a good moral diet in childhood. It is the practice of small acts of kindness that predispose the person to continuous acts of kindness as an adult.

Children need to practice their morality, just as a musician practices scales before playing a sonata or a ballplayer hones his skills in preparation for the game. No one learns to play the piano just by watching someone else play. The teacher sits beside the student, pointing out how to improve technique, correcting flaws. And you can't be taught gymnastics by watching an instructional video. You have to get on the balance beam yourself.

But what about virtue? Is learning good character like learning to eat properly or playing an instrument? The answer is mostly yes. Let's look at one virtue: courage. Courage is needed to act on one's convictions. It's possible to know what the right thing to do is but still not have the courage to do it.

If anyone should be concerned about courage and fostering it, it is the military. You can't have an army of cowards. The army requires its members to be willing to risk their lives, something foreign to our instinct for survival.

The military fashions courage from the material presented by ordinary men and women. Walking across a minefield is contrary to the instinct to preserve one's life. Running the other way and ducking for shelter is the sensible and natural thing to do when bullets start to fly. I remember that toward the end of my basic training at Fort Dix, after I had learned how to salute, repeat my general orders, make a bed, and shoot a rifle, we went to the field for night maneuvers. That day we were told what would happen and given instructions about what to do. We were told that as we went through the scrub brush in the dark, land mines would be detonated around us. The instructors drilled us again and again. "When there is an explosion, stay put! Wait to see what has happened. Assess the situation before you move." We knew exactly what to do.

Night fell and my company went looking for the mock enemy. As we walked down a sandy path into total darkness, there was a flash and a deafening explosion. My eyes were blinded, my ears were filled with the sound of my pumping heart. In an instant, every one of us bolted as fast and as far as our legs could carry us. Everything taught by day in the lecture hall evaporated in the face of panic. The sergeant called a halt to the war game and berated us for our foolish actions. He reiterated what he had said earlier. "Stay put!" The next time a mine went off nearby we did exactly that. Our fear hadn't disappeared, but it was under control. Having controlled our fear we could do what we were supposed to.

Whether we acquired real courage is an open question. We

may have gained what philosopher Alasdair MacIntyre calls a simulacrum of a virtue. He writes,

> *The well-trained soldier may do what courage would have demanded in a particular situation, but not because he is courageous but because he is well-trained or perhaps . . . because he is more frightened of his own officers than he is of the enemy. The genuinely virtuous agent however acts on the basis of a true and rational judgment.*

The army doesn't really care if it is the genuine article or not. They don't want soldiers cowering, for any reason. But even the military made a nod in the direction of making courage real by offering courses in civics. The point of the classes was to convince us that America was worth defending not simply on the basis of patriotism but on the grounds that democracy was good in and of itself. In other words, they tried to provide a rational basis for our actions.

Courage by itself isn't a moral good. Bungee jumping requires courage but it has nothing to do with morality. Some acts require bravery that encompass dangerous and immoral things, such as robbing a bank. Courage is an instrumental virtue, though, for without it we cannot act morally under trying circumstances. Without the ability to act in the face of danger, purported convictions ring hollow.

Acting cautiously makes sense most of the time. But there are occasions when morality requires putting ourselves on the line. And those who are most likely to act ethically even when they are putting themselves at risk are those who are in the habit of doing things for others.

Aristotle understood the connection between virtue (or vice), and habit. One's character, he wrote, is a matter of disposition. It is what we usually do, our typical way of behaving that matters. For Aristotle moral virtue is the habit of making right choices. The virtuous person is the one who makes the right choices and acts on those choices with regularity. It is the practice of making right choices most of the time that makes us virtuous.

At the turn of the twentieth century, American psychologist and philosopher William James concurred. In one of his lectures to teachers of psychology, he said,

> *See to it now, I beg you, that you make freemen of your pupils by habituating them to act, whenever possible, under the notion of a good. Get them habitually to tell the truth, not so much through showing them the wickedness of lying as by arousing their enthusiasm for honor and veracity. Wean them from their native cruelty by imparting to them some of your own positive sympathy with an animal's inner springs of joy.*

The correctness of Aristotle's and James's understanding of psychology is borne out by the lives of many of the rescuers of Jews. Their actions didn't arise spontaneously. A foundation had been laid before they were called on to risk themselves. As Fogelman writes, "It was not a whim that led these people to risk their lives and those of their families, but a response, almost a reflexive reaction in some cases, that came from core values developed and instilled in them in childhood."

One of the significant differences between the rescuers and the rest of the Germans was that rescuers were tolerant of differences and respected others. Rescuers also acquired the values of respect and tolerance in homes that treated them, as children, with respect. It was the specific application of the value during their childhood that made the difference. In Germany, as is true nearly everywhere, it was the unusual family that didn't say they valued love. Protestant and Catholic services spoke of Jesus' love and Teutonic myth making presented a love-filled world. The real difference in childrearing between those who became rescuers and those who were bystanders was which people were included in the circle of that love. For most, love was reserved for the family, the neighbor, the country—all defined in specific terms, terms that excluded those who didn't accept Christ, those who were defined as enemies of the state. Love alone doesn't make for humane values. What is important is whether the love is inclusive or exclusive, whether it draws circles to take people in or lines to keep them out, whether it is a source of self-satisfaction or whether it is a challenge. When the love extended to all people, not just those who shared their political views or religion or blood, then people were more likely to act on behalf of Jews and others in need. As Fogelman writes:

> In talking with rescuers from all kinds of different homes, I found that one quality above all others was emphasized time and again: a familial acceptance of people who were different. This value was the centerpiece of the childhood of rescuers and became the core from which their rescuer self evolved. From the earliest ages, their parents taught rescuers that people are inextricably linked to one another. No one person or group was better than any other. The conviction that all people, no matter how marginal, are of equal value was conveyed to children of both religious and nonreligious households.

When this inclusiveness was combined with feelings of self-worth, the chances that they would act as rescuers increased. "In fact," Fogelman writes, "many rescuers attributed their strength to their parents' love. Many felt themselves to be the adored favorite of one parent. . . . Indeed, I found that as children, many rescuers felt not only loved but protected."

Why would feeling loved incline one toward helping others? Psychologist Ervin Staub doesn't address rescuers per se but has studied the roots of prosocial behavior. His comments about the relationship between good feelings and helping shed light on the question. Apparently, experiences that create a positive mood increase helping. These experiences probably lessen self-focus and self-concern and thereby make people feel "richer" and in possession of greater resources, including time, energy, and competence. This makes giving and helping easier. Negative moods, or experiences that give rise to them, have more complex effects: They sometimes increase and sometimes decrease helping. The latter seems to happen when negative experiences lead to self-focus.

Positive self-esteem is a more stable source of such feelings. The evidence, although limited, does show that positive self-esteem is associated with helping behavior. Most rescuers report feeling close to their mothers and, on the whole, also report positively on their relationship to their fathers. Evidently, rescuers drew on the good memories of their childhoods to create a positive mood that outweighed the horrors they saw around them.

Moral habits—the disposition to choose moral values and to act on them consistently—are acquired from parents, relatives, friends, teachers, and a host of other sources in society.

One of the places in which people learn moral habits is their religious home. But the evidence that religious participation encourages people to become involved in activities that actually benefit the needy isn't very strong. An extensive study done by Princeton sociologist Robert Wuthnow concludes that the concerns of most churches are narrow:

> What the evidence on religious participation suggests is that churchgoing does not seem to generate convictions about caring that carry over into all realms of the believer's life. People do not, for example, see caring acted out in their churches and then go out with such conviction about the importance of caring that they help the next person they see. Instead, what they see and hear in church channels their caring. It is channeled, above all,

into programs the church as an organization is trying to promote. After this it is channeled informally among members and into certain kinds of traditionally accepted behaviors. One's definition of what constitutes a need and, when it is appropriate to care is, in short, shaped by the organization one attends.

From France comes an example of religious habits that are most noble. Not far from the French Alps, Andre and Magda Trocme, Edourad Theis and others in Le Chambon, descendants of Huguenots, were part of a tradition that identified with persecuted minorities. Their courageous actions were valorized in Philip Hallie's book *Lest Innocent Blood Be Shed: The Story of the Village of Le Chambon and How Goodness Happened There*. When Hallie, who was a professor of philosophy and humanities at Wesleyan College, first read an account of the villagewide rescue effort of Jewish children, he wrote:

That night when I lay on my back in bed with my eyes closed, I saw more clearly than ever the images that had made me weep. I saw two clumsy khaki-colored buses of the Vichy French pull into the village square. I saw the police captain facing the pastor of the village and warning him that if he did not give up the names of the Jews he had been sheltering in the village, he and his fellow pastors, as well as the families who had been caring for the Jews, would be arrested. I saw the pastor refuse to give up these people who had been strangers in his village, even at the risk of his own destruction. Then I saw the only Jew the police could find, sitting in an otherwise empty bus. I saw a thirteen-year-old boy, the son of the pastor, pass a piece of his precious chocolate through the window to the prisoner, while twenty gendarmes who were guarding the lone prisoner watched. And then I saw the villagers passing their little gifts through the window until there were gifts all around him—most of the food in those hungry days during the German occupation of France.

The people of Le Chambon bear out Buddha's statement that "the deed develops into habit and habit hardens into character." The villagers were inspired by their religion but they also regularly put their convictions into action. Le Chambon had a history of sheltering the needy. At the turn of the twentieth century, the villagers cared for sickly children; in the 1930s the citizens opened their doors to refugees from the Spanish Civil War. So when in 1940 a Jewish refugee had knocked on Magda Trocme's kitchen door, she opened it and without hesitation took in the stranger. In the documentary *Weapons of the Spirit* about Le Chambon's rescue of five thousand Jews, the filmmaker Pierre Sauvage asks a couple why they risked their lives for children they didn't know. The couple says nothing for a moment, then answers, "We were used to it."

Magda's husband, Andre, was the pastor in the village. He preached an austere but complex Christianity based on Jesus as the exemplar of sacrificial love. The pastor was a man

who has an eye and a heart for the individuality of people like no man I have ever met. It was the humane warmth of Trocme, his openness to fresh feelings and ideas, that made him the man to lead a place of refuge whose purpose was not only to save the lives of children but also to set an example of overcoming evil with good.

He preached that the most dangerous people were the "decent" ones who stayed on the sidelines, either out of cowardice or indifference, when innocent people were being humiliated and destroyed. The villagers, pious in their religion, listened carefully and followed Andre and Magda's lead. They, too, had incorporated the belief that Christianity required preventing harm and doing good. As the Trocme's daughter said, they were taught "the importance of doing what was right, and learned to listen to our own conscience. We saw our parents disobey the law and were taught that a system that persecutes *must* be disobeyed." So the village itself became a haven for Jewish refugees, mainly children. By the time of the liberation, thousands of refugees had found safety and protection in Le Chambon.

When our values are true, then habits help us make moral decisions easily. We don't need to wonder whether or not to help a drowning person. If we are expert swimmers, we jump in. If not, we run for help immediately. But when our habits are badly formed, we hesitate, uncertain what to do. We wait too long. The person drowns. Or if we have not learned to love the right values, we may walk away.

Habits, however, are tricky. If we acquire them without having learned to be critical thinkers, we become the kind of person that the twelfth-century Jewish philosopher Moses Maimonides wrote about when he said, "Men like the opinions to which they have been accustomed from their youth; they defend them, and shun contrary views: and this is one of the things that prevents men from finding truth, for they cling to the opinions of habit."

There are also habits that once were useful but no longer are. Between my house and Jericho Turnpike there are two stop signs. These signs, near an elementary school, have been there at least as long as I have been living in Westbury—more than twenty-five years. Although no car drive is so routine that I could do it blindfolded, two decades on a less-than-one-mile strip comes close to it. So without much thought I start to slow down a half block before each sign, come to a halt, then proceed.

The trouble is that a short while ago one of the signs was moved a block closer to the school. Still, as I travel along the road, I slow down where the sign used to be; and occasionally, when my mind isn't fully focused on driving, I stop where there is no stop sign. This old habit is now dangerous. Not long ago a car passed my stopped car as I stood still, waiting for a car from the side street to enter the main road. This nearly caused an accident, as my stopping there appeared senseless. What once served me as almost second nature now is an impediment to good driving. I need new habits.

Habits can make us lazy. We go about as though sleepwalking. Habits cannot replace vigilance. We make errors when we aren't paying attention. The trick is putting together both moral reflection and moral habit. "The integration of habit and reflection joins together the various intellectual and active ways that one can respond to a moral event," writes William Damon, professor of education and one of the country's leading experts on moral education. "The reflective judgment lends support and perspective to the habit, and the habitual reaction lends substance and shape to the reflection. This makes a powerful combination, one that is both effective and inspiring."

Reason is the basis for moral habits, moral habits require critical thinking. One without the other is like expecting a one-legged person to become a long-distance runner. It is possible, but very difficult.

21.

Provide Opportunities for Your Children to Help Others

Question: How do you know what virtue is? The answer, given by Aristotle, is, find a virtuous person and watch what he does.

Now here's another question: How do you get to Carnegie Hall? Answer: Practice! Practice! Practice!

These two questions and answers capture an essential truth about how ethical people get to be that way. The odds are greatly increased that Jennifer and Kevin will grow up to be moral if they are shown examples of moral behavior and they are given the opportunities to practice their ethics.

Ethical behavior is similar to other skills—playing an instrument, being an athlete or artist, racing car driver or baker. Being around people who love music increases the chances that someone will be a musician; exposure to sports makes it more likely that someone will engage in athletics herself.

So Kevin sings and Jennifer picks up a ball. They will do this all by themselves and may very well be involved with other children who share the same interests. If they really want to improve their skills, though, they will have to commit time to develop them. There may be lessons or simply hour after hour working with paper and paint or months on end of throwing a ball through a hoop. At some point, practice gives way to skill and Kevin can sing unself-consciously and Jennifer plays basketball as though on automatic pilot.

Kindness, consideration, generosity, and other virtues can become second nature, too. As a parent, you may have to provide opportunities for your children to help others—just as you may have to buy sneakers and arrange for league play for Jennifer—to build on the interest they already have. Many opportunities present themselves: visiting a sick friend, shopping for a person who is homebound, tutoring in a subject she knows well.

Schools around the country now require community work. This is a good thing, as long as it is clear that the reason for the volunteer work is because there are people in need, not because it looks good on the school record.

Being a moral person means *acting* morally. More than empathy, more than motivation, more than judging well, being a moral person means doing the right thing when called on. Ethics is behavior, and like all behavior, it requires practice.

The connection between habits and ethical behavior has been well understood. For a thousand years, Chinese students would recite a poem at the beginning of the schoolday. It reflected an attitude toward life, one that confirmed the good deeds of people and recognized that we become more ethical as time goes on as we practice our morality over and over. The poem reads:

> *People are originally*
> *Endowed with a nature which is all good.*
> *And therefore by nature people are all alike.*
> *It is practice that makes the divergence.*
> *If they are not properly taught,*
> *Their nature will be thwarted.*

22.

Give Positive Verbal and Nonverbal Feedback for Being a Good Person

We assume that acting morally as an adult will come naturally to those who have been raised on a good moral diet in childhood. It is the practice of small acts of kindness that predispose the person to continual—not random—acts of kindness as an adult.

Your children need for you to tell them that they have done the right thing. They need to experience it from the way you look at them, the way you touch them. Nothing is worse than to get inconsistent and contradictory messages. A parent who, on the one hand says, "I love you," and on the other, turns away when her child tries to kiss her sends mixed messages.

Another inconsistency is to say one thing and do another. I am reminded of the story of a friend of mine, Alan. He has strong opinions about what the right thing is: be honest, help those in need, support the causes you believe in. When he goes camping, he makes certain to follow all the rules about keeping to the trail, putting out campfires, not littering, and so forth.

As an example of his honesty, once when he went shopping at a department store, he realized that he had been given five dollars too much in change. He wrote a letter to the store's headquarters and included a five-dollar check.

One day he and his son Richard, then fourteen, were out together. Alan parallel parked his station wagon and in so doing scraped the car in front of him. When he got out, he looked at the other car and walked away.

"What are you doing, Dad?" Richard asked. "Aren't you going to leave a note or something?"

"No," Alan said. "Did you see that car? It already was full of scratches and dents."

"That has nothing to do with it," Richard insisted. "You scratched it, so you should do something."

Alan said that his one scratch was really minor and made no difference. The owner wouldn't even notice. Leaving a note would make a big deal out of nothing.

Richard shook his head. He seemed to be saying, "How could you, Dad? I thought you were ethical."

The incident made Alan think about his own conduct and he used the incident to examine himself. He also used it as an opportunity to talk to Richard about moral rules and the need for judgment when applying those rules. He talked to his son about the difference between big offences and minor ones and the importance of forgiving someone who makes a mistake. As a young child, Richard didn't really understand the distinctions Alan was making.

Both Alan and Richard learned something that day. Alan discovered how easy it is to rationalize unethical behavior. Richard learned that not all indiscretions are the same.

23.

Work with Your Children in Community and Volunteer Service

"I don't want to help," Jennifer says when she comes home complaining about having to do community service. You are reluctant to force her to do it anyway. You remember the joke about the Boy Scout who helped the old lady across the street. The problem was that the old lady didn't *want* to cross the street.

Many religious and service institutions, and some school districts provide opportunities for volunteer service for children. Take advantage of these; encourage your children to get involved in community affairs. Such activities expose Jennifer to the larger world in which she lives. It helps establish a perspective about her own life, as it exposes her to the lives of those who are different from her.

"I want to stay home," Kevin says. He'd rather play ball than help the hungry. Even if Kevin goes to a soup kitchen because it looks good on his school record or Jennifer volunteers at the nursing home because all her friends are doing it, the very act of doing a good deed, even for the wrong reasons, is helpful for building up the habits of ethical behavior.

I agree with the rabbi, who once said, "A person should always occupy himself with doing good, even if for the wrong reasons, for eventually it will be for the right reason." When I was in grammar school, once a month was "bank day." I had a passbook savings account and week after week I added a dime to the account. I would rather have spent the dime on an ice-cream cone. But I didn't have a choice. My mother gave me the dime and looked at my passbook when I got home. Throughout my adult life I have still had the habit of deferring some pleasures to put a small amount of money in my savings. The advice given by financial planners today was instilled in me as a child: pay yourself first. My parents had established the habit of saving for the future that has served me well.

Similarly, helping others at a young age establishes the habit of being responsible for lives other than your own. A family I know takes the Passover seder as an opportunity to contribute to a worthy cause. One year, the parents asked their ten-year-old son to do some research and he came back with the suggestion of supporting a private nonprofit home for young mothers with children who have AIDS. During the service, participants talked about how they could best support that organization.

Many families participate in walk-a-thons, work in soup kitchens, clean up community gardens, build houses for poor people, and so on. The list is endless.

In my family, we have a ritual activity at Christmastime. Each December, Amnesty International conducts a Holiday Greetings campaign. The Nobel Prize–winning organization sends to its members the names of prisoners of conscience—people imprisoned because of their religion, beliefs, or other noncriminal activities. After we open our presents, the adults in the family send cards with messages of peace and good wishes to those prisoners throughout the world. Our grandchildren help out at their level—they lick stamps, place the cards in the envelopes, and put the envelopes in a pile. The activity takes about a half hour. The next day, the grandchildren often accompany one of us to the post office to mail the cards.

If you can do something for others together as a family, so much the better. You, then, aren't expecting more of your child than you are of yourself.

24.

Expect and Encourage Good Deeds from Your Children

Expectations are very powerful things. They can work either positively or negatively. We know this from a number of studies, especially in schools where teachers play such an important role in children's lives. The most famous study is described in *Pygmalian in the Classroom* and was conducted by psychologist Robert Rosenthal. Children were divided randomly at the beginning of the year, but some teachers were told that they had the bright students and other teachers were told they had the slow learners. At the end of the year the students were evaluated. Teachers who had the "bright" class thought the children were wonderful. Those who had the "slow" class claimed their children were difficult. Even more telling, it turned out that, on the whole, the students who were labeled "slow" didn't perform as well as those who were labeled "smart." In other words, students' performance lived up to teachers' expectations. (Whether the study itself was an ethical one is another matter.)

This is known as a self-fulfilling prophecy and it is more common than we think. The reason for it is that, to some degree, we take our cues from others; and what we require and demand of ourselves is partly a response to what others have expected and demanded from us. We are always under the influence of other people and are reacting to them in one way or another.

Expectations aren't everything, but they do count for a lot. So if you expect your children to be generous, they often are. If you think that they are inconsiderate, they will often turn out to be that way.

But if you expect that Kevin will act responsibly, if you expect Jennifer to act thoughtfully, you increase the chances that they will develop those good habits. Children often live up to—or down to—the expectations of adults. This isn't always true, of course. And I am also talking about a long-term process, something that begins in early childhood. We really don't know if we are successful or not until Kevin and Jennifer are adults. Along the way, there are bound to be times in which we think we have failed. Kevin will be irresponsible and Jennifer will be thoughtless. But remember, we are talking about acquiring habits. If our children were always responsible and thoughtful from the very beginning, you wouldn't need this book.

I believe that if you expect and encourage good deeds from your children, your children are likely to rise to the occasion when it really matters. If they admire you, they want to please you. And if you are open about what you value and why, they will know what habits are worth developing. And once having become habituated to doing good, they will continue, if only to please themselves.

25.

Help Your Children Keep Promises

Promise keeping is a prime virtue, for without it we couldn't live with other people. We have to count on people doing what they say they will do. There are legal contracts to enforce business transactions, and there are marriage vows to bind families together. Still, most of the time we don't resort to such formality to make sure that someone keeps her word. We simply take it for granted that most of the time most people will do all in their power to keep their promises.

Promise keeping is essential for social life to continue. It will take time for Kevin and Jennifer to learn this lesson. But before they do, they will occasionally break their promises for self-serving purposes. Remember, at the early stages of moral reasoning, until about eight years old, children can't truly recognize the interests and needs of others. They experience the world through their own egocentric point of view. If they tell the truth, it is because they want to avoid being punished or they want to be rewarded. And if they keep their promises, it is because they believe it is a moral rule and it is a good one because parents and other authority figures stand behind it.

By the time Jennifer and Kevin are about sixteen, they will understand the world in a very different way from the way they did when they were very young. Now they realize that moral rules exist not because someone has dictated them into creation but because they are necessary to keep society going and are beneficial. No longer egocentric, they, as adolescents, can stand outside themselves and take a view of society as a whole.

The interesting thing about moral development is that much of it unfolds more or less naturally. This means that even if you had never talked to Jennifer about the importance of keeping promises, she would have gotten the message from her friends and playmates. Her little world also rests on trust, and the games she plays and her friendships would fail if promise keeping weren't present.

Prejudice

Treating All People Fairly Is Fundamental to Morality

> When the heart feels sympathy for the oppressed, it has been touched by grace.
>
> —ED YOUNG

No one is born being prejudiced; it must be learned. At least that is the conventional wisdom. For example, in Rodgers and Hammerstein's musical drama *South Pacific*, a naval officer reflects on his own reluctance to marry a Balinese woman whom he loves. Realizing that he harbors racist sentiments, he sings "You've got to be taught before it's too late / Before you are six or seven or eight / To hate all the people your relatives hate / You've got to be carefully taught." These lyrics present a popular view that if children were raised in a society unburdened by prejudice and bigotry, they would meet the world without bias or hatred.

The idea is right in one respect but wrong in another. If we mean that there is nothing natural about hating one another simply because of sex or religion or color or language, then it is true. There is nothing natural about being a bigot. But in another sense we form our biases all by ourselves, and in that way being prejudiced is quite natural.

Let me explain.

The ability and the desire to discriminate is built into us from birth. Indeed, human beings cannot do without it. It is an important survival skill. We need to sort one thing from another: safe foods from poisonous ones, sharp objects from blunt ones, pleasure from pain. Infants recognize the difference between mother and father, friends from strangers. Your infant presses her small body against yours because you are familiar. At the same time she is wary of those she doesn't know. Familiarity breeds contentment because it feels safe. Your child probably falls asleep more easily in his own bed than an unfamiliar one because he knows the noises of his own home and the smell of his sheets.

By discriminating between this thing and that thing, children put like things with like. Your daughter sorts her dolls according to size. Your son stacks his blocks according to shape. Without this ability, children would be placed in great peril. They would eat plastic foam peanuts and wander off with strangers. So the ability to discriminate is an essential survival skill. A child or adult who cannot distinguish between helpful and harmful things would be in great trouble.

You may have noticed the way your children categorize things around them spontaneously. Their minds are structured in such a way that they put what they think of as like objects—objects that seemingly possess the same properties—together. Before they are two, children are distinguishing between circles and triangles, blue from red. By age three children are sorting trucks from cars, big dolls from little ones, men and boys, women and girls. This sorting process isn't imposed on children by society. It isn't socialization—knowing something because someone has taught it. Categorizing this way happens to children everywhere, whatever their culture. Socialization comes later, is layered on top of this natural cognitive process.

Jean Piaget noted that between the ages of six and ten, children engage in what he calls "concrete operational thought." The concrete thinker creates fixed categories. If something comes along that challenges the system (that is, something doesn't fit into a category), then an exception is made for that instance alone. If someone has the wrong-headed idea that Puerto Ricans are a group of people he can't befriend but then meets a Puerto Rican he likes, the experience does not necessarily destroy the prejudice. The concrete thinker can't restructure categories, he can only make exceptions. On the other hand, the person who can think "formally" can transcend categories and create new ones. The ability to transcend fixed categories allows for the possibility of overcoming negative stereotypes.

So, if part of being moral is being tolerant, then we have to encourage children to move from concrete to formal thinking. This isn't always easy to do, for moving from one stage to the next can be threatening. Concrete thinking brings order to chaos. It puts people and things in place and keeps them there. It makes the world understandable and safe.

But life frequently presents challenges that become opportunities to move forward. Because as soon as the categories are created, they are threatened by external events. Ten-year-olds are acutely aware of their bodies and want to know about physical limits. They want to know how many bones, muscles, cells, gallons of blood, and miles of intestines a person has. They are also intensely concerned with wanting to know what happens if I get sick, break a bone, drink alcohol, or smoke cigarettes. As psychologist Robert Kegan writes, "order, regularity, and stability of the world give the child the capacity to master it in a way never before possible. This mastery is threatened by unpredictability, and questions that ask 'What if . . . ?' are seeking not only information but control."

Even as adults we continue to process information this way. Socrates and Aristotle used the method of systematizing and classifying as a means of better understanding the world. "Socrates taught," philosopher John Dewey wrote, "that no matter how confusing the situation might be, [people] could, by diligent searching, discerning common elements among diversities." Socrates tried to find common patterns in the many things, morals included, that he and his students argued about. Aristotle's method of thinking is derived from Socrates'. Both were concerned with bringing "order out of confusion, system out of chaos."

Categorization is also important because it is a shortcut method of learning. We don't have to reinvent the wheel every time we have to get from point A to point B. By creating classes of objects, we know that most things like this (say, ripe vegetables) are good for us when we put them in our mouths, most things like that (say, rotten vegetables) are bad for us when we swallow them. We don't have to eat every rotting vegetable we encounter to know that putrid food makes us sick or swallow every rock to know that it is indigestible. This knowing is prejudice, literally "prejudging." We make a judgment about something without actually knowing it firsthand because we have had an experience of something like it before. Discrimination leads to prejudging and this, in turn, leads to generalizations. Generalizing from one instance to others is an essential part of learning. All this happens naturally as our cognitive abilities develop over time and with the right stimulation.

Distinguishing, categorizing, and discriminating are essential to morality. It is a double-edged sword, though. On the one side, it is the source of judgment; and as I explained earlier, reason and judgment are tied together. Judging one thing better than another is what we mean by valuing or prizing. When you say that you want to teach your child values, what you mean is that you want them to value one thing more than other. There can be no ethics without such appraisals. We couldn't say this person is a good person if we had no ability to distinguish between good and bad. There would be no praise and no condemnation for anything done. Discrimination also has its limitations. For one thing, when we classify something, we sometimes don't see what is truly there. For example, Aristotle defined slaves as animated tools and grouped them not with human beings but with animals and plants. This then became a justification for slavery. Because slaves weren't human by definition, there was no need to be concerned about their freedom or well-being. The problem, then, is that when we generalize we can easily make the mistakes, putting people into categories in which they don't belong.

Of course, there is a difference between being discriminating and being bigoted, but you can see how one can lead to the other. My point is that we all have prejudices but that prejudice can either be positive or negative. We can either be prejudiced in favor of something or be prejudiced against something. For example, growing up as I did, I was predisposed to think of New Yorkers as more interesting and somehow "better" people than other Americans. It wasn't that all of us from New York necessarily shared the same interests. Rather it was that I expected that somehow because they came from New York they possessed the qualities that made for the kind of person that I considered worthwhile.

By itself there is nothing wrong with this. The problem isn't that prejudice predisposes us to like some things over others. We are born with the propensity to categorize and, therefore, to be prejudiced. Categorizing is natural and universal behavior, but which groups of people we are prejudiced against is a matter of socialization. A useful way of thinking about this process is to compare it to walking. Children don't need to be taught to walk. All things being equal, children learn how to walk and would walk even if they never saw another human being to imitate. Infants move from sitting to crawling to walking somewhere during their first year because this is what human beings do. So all children walk; but the manner in which we walk is partly a matter of socialization. For instance, the walk of the Maasai in East Africa is quite distinctive. It is a kind of loping, a long stride with a bounce. That the Maasai walk is natural; the loping is cultural. In some cultures, people stride, in others they take small steps.

Negative social prejudices are the problem. These biases can lead us to discriminate against others, then to be intolerant, and finally to become bigots. So what is it that takes us from prejudice as a helpful tool in dealing with the world to prejudice as bigotry?

For one, positive and negative bigotry can be opposite sides of the same coin. When your child identifies with her school, she may well think that children who go to other schools aren't as good as her fellow students. By viewing an entire group of people—in my case, New Yorkers—as interesting, I viewed everyone else as a little less worthy. Abraham Kaplan says this kind of prejudice comes from an error in logic. It is what he calls "the fallacy of comparison," the mistake in believing that the worth of one group must always be compared to that of another, thereby making one group better and the other worse. It is hard to remember that differences are merely distinguishing; one group isn't necessarily better than the other.

As common as the fallacy of comparison is, most social biases don't come from faulty logic. Here is where conventional thinking about prejudice is correct. Bigotry is most often the result of teaching and imitation. No one is born a racist. Children see color but they don't necessarily associate one race as good and another as bad. This must be learned. No one is born an anti-Semite. Children know that people have different religions. But hating a particular religion must be taught.

There are often historical and social factors in society that form the mold in which bigotry takes hold. Unfortunately, racism is still present today. As a parent, it is useful to keep this in mind because your child may well be exposed to these same bigotries in school and on the playground.

Competition

There is much evidence that points to an increase in bias and bigotry when people are forced to compete. When Chinese immigrants took part in the California gold rush, for example, they were called bloodthirsty and inhuman, unfair competitors. A decade later their efforts were essential in building the transcontinental railroad. No longer barbarians, they were now described as trustworthy and intelligent. Many immigrant groups faced similar experiences. If those already in the country thought that the newcomers threatened their jobs, immigrants were stereotyped negatively. If instead immigrants were seen as necessary to perform low-status and undesirable jobs, they were viewed as welcome contributors to the American scene. Even today, immigrants are welcome in one part of the country because they fill gaps in the labor force, embracing low-paying jobs, or are unwelcome in areas where they are viewed as taking jobs away from residents.

In some ways, schools and homes are places where children compete for scarce resources. Your daughter may strive to earn the best grades in the class or perhaps she wants to be the most popular. In fact, only one person can be the *most* popular and only one pupil can have the *best* grades. And you find yourself not being able to give her all the attention she wants because of the demands of other children or work. Then she feels disappointed and frustrated and may displace her unhappiness in what feels like a safer channel. If she doesn't get these things, she is more likely to develop prejudices against others than if she got what she wanted. So now she dislikes boys or children from the next town. Those who are frustrated and feel deprived tend to displace their feelings onto others by developing negative attitudes toward them. They will pick out traits that are less than perfect, exaggerate them, and then generalize to an entire group of people.

Bigotry is likely to surface when your child feels that he hasn't gotten what he (or others like him) deserves. Then he feels resentful and is more likely to focus on the hurt rather than on righting the condition. When your child thinks of himself as the injured party and believes that there isn't much that he can do to change his situation, he is likely to become resentful, jealous, and angry. This frustration may well be turned outward toward others who are defenseless. A number of laboratory experiments support this idea. In one study cited by psychologist Ervin Staub, two groups stated their opinions about various minorities. In return for their completing a questionnaire, subjects were promised free passes to a movie. When the first group was done, the experimenter told them that they couldn't go to the movie and instead had to complete a second and somewhat difficult task. The second group went to the movies. Subjects in the first group were, not surprisingly, disappointed and frustrated. Finally, both groups were asked to restate their opinions about the minority groups they had commented on in the original questionnaire. Interestingly, whatever negative attitudes toward those minority groups the first group had expressed initially had intensified by the end of the process. They disliked certain minority groups more, even though the groups had nothing whatsoever to do with their frustration. The second group, which hadn't been frustrated, didn't change its attitudes toward minority groups.

Parents and teachers need to be aware that children who have been frustrated will harden their prejudices against groups they don't like.

Stability

There are also larger social conditions that affect the development of prejudices. Americans tend to move around a great deal—they change jobs, they buy new houses, they get divorced, and they remarry. These all take a toll on children. Children need stability in their lives, a setting in which it is safe to try out new ways of thinking and behaving. They need to be able to count on some things staying the same. Of course, that isn't always possible. Loved ones die, economic pressures force people to move, and there may be good reason for parents to separate. These circumstances present serious challenges to your child's moral development because he feels he has little control over what is happening to him.

Some who study the moral development of children draw a link between parents and society. Staub writes that "it is necessary that parents have relatively ordered and secure life circumstances. If the basic needs for food, shelter, health care, and emotional support are unfulfilled, and if [parents] lack a feeling of reasonable control over their lives" they aren't likely to relate positively to their children. Staub continues, "When unemployment increases, reports of child abuse increase, and periods of economic problems are associated with increased societal violence."

No change by itself needs to be overwhelming. You can increase the chances that your child will cope well with these changes if she isn't kept in the dark. Talk to her and explain what is happening. A simple explanation is all that is needed for a young child. Older children need reasons along with explanations. Don't ask her advice, because that's likely only to add to the anxiety. Changes that you may see as positive may not be seen that way by your child. A bigger house or better neighborhood, for example, may not be what she wants. She'd rather have her familiar room and old friends. If you can take your child's point of view, you can help her feel more secure about the changes.

Existing Prejudices

Dealing with the prejudices in society can be difficult. Sometimes biases exist all around us, and we absorb negative attitudes as though they were perfectly reasonable. I am dismayed by the prejudices I unwittingly hold. For years I thought nothing of referring to "flesh-colored" bandages, when the truth is that calling a peach-colored bandage "flesh" presumes that white skin tone is the norm. It never occurred to me how biased such a label was, and I thought nothing of perpetuating the stereotype.

If an entire society believes that others are inferior, then prejudice becomes the standard for behavior. Bias doesn't have to be (and often isn't) rooted in anything real. Sometimes the prejudice hasn't anything to do with the person who is the object of the prejudice. When I was in Changchun, Manchuria, I met an exchange student from Zanzibar. I asked him what it was like being one of only a handful of blacks in a city of three million people. We were in the lounge of my hotel, and when he saw a Chinese person sitting nearby he was reluctant to speak freely. I suggested that we speak in Swahili. Only when we spoke in an African language—and he was certain no one else could understand what he had to say—could he tell me what was on his mind. He explained to me that he was eager to return home. He was a track star for the polytechnic institute; but when he left the track, he might as well have been invisible. Banners waved for him when he ran, but not once during his five years there had he been invited into a Chinese home. Students avoided him in the cafeteria. Lauded as an athlete, he was shunned as an individual.

Several years later, on another trip to China, I met with a group of local university students. I was curious about the exchange student's experience and asked my hosts about Africans in Beijing.

"There are students from Africa at our university," one of the students told me. He then volunteered, "We don't like them, though." The others assented.

"Why not?" I asked.

He told me that there had been problems.

"Africans are disrespectful of Chinese women," he said.

"Why do you say that?"

"Once there was a party and Chinese women were raped by them."

"When did this happen?" I asked.

"Oh, a while ago," he said. "Maybe ten years." A little later he told me that the alleged incident took place in Shanghai, nearly a thousand miles away.

These Chinese students didn't like Africans because of what they had heard happened a decade before, at the other end of the country. They didn't like Africans because of what they defined as the Africans' uncontrollable violence and sexual appetites. The disposition to see Africans this way fit in easily with the traditional Asian depiction of the devil as black.

Prejudice can also arise from conforming to group attitudes. When we don't think for ourselves, we simply repeat the patterns of prejudice that exist in society. I'm thinking, for example, of the bias that we have in America against plumpness in women. Being slender is prized by many women, no matter how old, no matter what their body type. In Africa, it is just the opposite. One year I went to Kenya with a friend of mine who is very thin. When we were visiting my friends Joshua and Raili Ongesa, my friend was invited to Raili's cooking house, a place reserved only for women. The room was dark, filled with the smoke from an open fire on which women were boiling tea with milk and sugar. Then they took my friend by her hand and stood her in the center of the room. They walked around her, touching her long blond hair, feeling her body. They talked among themselves in the local language, Gusii. "We want to know, are you sick?" asked one who spoke English.

She assured them she wasn't. Why did they think she was?

"Because you are so skinny." The Kenyan spoke to her friends in Gusii again. They shook their heads. "So," the woman continued, "if you aren't sick, then your husband must be mistreating you. You aren't poor. You are an American. So tell your husband to feed you better."

In America you can't be too rich or too thin. In Kenya, at least until recently, you couldn't be too rich or too fat.

Once after visiting a friend in the hospital on Long Island, I remarked that I noticed something for the first time: doctors wearing sandals. "Without socks?" my friend asked. "That's going too far. It's too casual. And dirty, too." I then told her that it was women doctors I was talking about, and suddenly her attitude changed. In her mind the doctors were men. When she learned that the doctors referred to were women, she also changed her mind about the sandals. She had no problem with women doctors wearing sandals. And for the sake of consistency, men wearing them no longer appalled her. She learned about two prejudices by my one chance remark.

And it was in that same hospital that I discovered another one of my own prejudices. As an elevator door opened, in stepped a young black woman wearing sneakers and a punk hairdo. I was certain she was a orderly, until she turned so I could read her name tag. She was a doctor, and so out the window went my unconscious prejudice that doctors are male, white, older, and conservatively dressed and coifed.

Group Pressure

Every one of us belongs to groups. We have families, friends, and neighbors. Being part of such communities is what makes us human. But sometimes being part of a group presents a problem. Your daughter may question herself when all her friends think there is nothing wrong with deliberately hurting an opponent on the soccer field to score a goal. Or your son may think that it's okay to cheat on a test because all his friends are doing it. It takes independence of heart and mind to hold steadfast to moral beliefs when they aren't shared by the group.

Occasionally, the pressure to do the wrong thing is obvious. But the pressure to conform can also be subtle. One study showed that negative attitudes increase when someone overhears a derogatory comment about a racial or ethnic group. Subjects were given a transcript from a criminal trial. The case involved a white defendant who was represented by a black lawyer. The lawyer's photograph was appended to the tran-

script. While the subjects were reading the transcript, two people, confederates of the researcher, walked by. They called the
lawyer a shyster and then used a racial epithet to describe him.
When they walked near another group of subjects, they referred
to the lawyer as a shyster again. This time they made no reference to his race. The researchers then asked the subjects their
opinion of the competence of the lawyer in the case. Those who
heard the racial slur rated him lower than those who only heard
him called a shyster. Because the only difference between the
two groups was that one heard a derogatory comment about
the lawyer's race, the researchers concluded that race alone was
enough to account for the lower rating given to him by that
group.

Resisting peer pressure is especially difficult for adolescents,
as they move from the intimate setting of the family and local
school. Joining groups is natural for teenagers, because this allows them to move away from their own families and form an
independent identity. For this reason, they become susceptible
to conforming to the group for the sake of fitting in. This "back-
sliding" from independence to dependence on the group is generally temporary. But for some, it becomes the final stage in
which prejudice becomes bigotry.

Psychologists have found that people who are bigots as a
rule come from homes characterized by harsh and threatening
discipline, homes in which parents often withdrew their love as
a form of discipline. As a result, children were insecure and
depended highly on the parent. They were frightened children.
"This combination," psychologist Eliot Aronson writes, "sets
the stage for the emergence of an adult with a high degree of
anger, which, because of fear and insecurity, takes the form of
displaced aggression against powerless groups, while the individual maintains respect for authority."

26.

Examine Your Own Biases

Your children learn from observation and often imitate what they see. So if you have biases, they probably will too. This means that you need to examine your own prejudices so your children won't acquire the limitations with which you live.

"But I'm a fair-minded person," you might protest. Although this is undoubtedly true, the fact is that we all have prejudices of one form or another. They are impossible to escape. Every one of us benefits from and is bedeviled by the way the mind puts things together, as well as the prejudices built into the society in which we live. We may have subtle biases against people whose race is different or who do a different type of work. Your child will quickly see beyond your stated ethical principles to what you really believe.

It is difficult for us to rid ourselves of social prejudices because they come so easily to us. One of the curious things about human beings is that whatever group we identify with, we think of ourselves as living correctly and consider outsiders as somewhat less human. It is hard to shake this. Of course, the group we identify with is pretty much arbitrary. Once we get beyond parents and children, we draw our circles not because there is anything natural about them, but because that is the way our culture has taught us to see. Do we identify with others because of our sex, religion, race, ethnicity, nationality, class, or political philosophy? For some, the circle is wide; and for others, it is relatively small. But everyone's circle has limits, and it takes deliberate effort to widen it.

Often we are only dimly aware of all we are really thinking or feeling. One of the great advances of psychology has been the recognition that much of our lives are lived on an unconscious level. In fact, there are times that our real feelings and thoughts are contrary to what we think we are feeling, thinking, or even doing. We are much like an iceberg, the exposed portion is only a small part of the whole. And because we all want to think well of ourselves, we often refuse to look at the parts of ourselves that are negative but present nevertheless.

So it is important in raising a moral child to stop periodically and examine your own unspoken assumptions. If you fail to do this, as your children grow older they will be all too aware of the discrepancy between what you say you value and what in fact you do. Given the choice between doing what you tell them to do and following your example, most children go straight past the words. Ask yourself questions such as: Do I have friends of different races, religions, or classes? If not, why not? Am I comfortable when I find myself as a minority in a group? Are there any minority groups living in my neighborhood? How do I feel when I see someone from one of those groups walking on my street? When I hear about crime, before I see a picture of the person arrested, what do I imagine the person to look like?

Acknowledging our own negative attitudes is a first step to softening our prejudices. This will help us match our words with our deeds and clarify the lessons we really want to teach our children.

27.

Provide Examples That Counteract Society's Prejudices

It is a great shock when you hear your children saying unkind things about groups of people when you yourself have never said such things. Where did they ever get such awful thoughts?

The sources are endless. They can get them from their peers, from television, from the movies, from books, or from the Internet. There is so much bias and stereotyping that it really isn't surprising that they pick it up somewhere.

But even if somehow your children could be spared society's biases, they may still find themselves a part of one group that dislikes another. Maybe it is the jocks or the nerds or the kids who listen to folk music or those who like heavy metal.

It isn't surprising that children will sort people into various groups and then make value judgments about them. Of course, left to themselves, these social categories may be very different from the ones society deems important. Their distinctions may not be based, for example, on skin color but on the color of eyes, not language but whether one prefers hot dogs to hamburgers. Children will always find ways of creating insiders and outsiders, where the people who they identify with are thought to be somehow superior.

When children do this, it is relatively easy for us to help them overcome these biases. Mostly, they will outgrow them just as they do their clothes. But a mild comment, such as "Suzanne is a girl, just like you," helps to speed along that process.

But when the categories are not created by them but inherited from the society at large, our work becomes harder and our efforts need to be persistent, deliberate, and long term.

I remember many years ago when my then five-year-old son said that he didn't like brown people very much. They didn't seem very nice to him.

"Well, who don't you like?" my wife asked him.

He mentioned one of the boys in the neighborhood.

"He likes to fight a lot," Eric explained.

Was there anyone else he didn't like?

He couldn't think of any.

We then asked him about his nursery school and reminded him of some of the boys he played with there. Some were white, some brown. He mentioned two or three schoolmates who fought a lot and he didn't like them either.

They weren't brown people.

We then asked him the names of the children he did like.

"Roger and Wayne," he said. They lived next door.

They are brown.

And we mentioned Eric's sister, our adopted daughter Kori, who is also brown. He likes her, he said, but sometimes he doesn't like her.

I think this little conversation (and others like it along the way) helped add a corrective to society's prevailing stereotype.

28.

Don't Allow Biased or Bigoted Comments to Go Unchallenged

You're standing on line with your child at the supermarket and the person in front of you makes a bigoted remark. What do you do?

If you say nothing, there is the risk that Kevin will think that such remarks are acceptable. But they aren't. Although people are entitled to their beliefs, you know that such comments are inaccurate, inappropriate, and hurtful. You know that the record has to be set straight, that Kevin needs to know that you don't share the prejudice.

The easiest (but not the best) thing to do when confronted with an unbidden remark is let it slide. Kevin has heard worse—or at least he will. Yet if you say nothing, in some small way you become part of the problem. In Kevin's eyes, such remarks can't be too bad if you have no objections to them. After all, when he does or says something you don't like, you say something about it. So he may take your silence as approval.

The problem really is not whether to challenge the comment but whether to do it on the spot or to wait to do it in a different way. To respond publicly requires courage, and it may not be the wisest thing. That person you challenge may be irrational and dangerous. Although there are times to take risks, this may not be one of them.

If the person making the comment isn't a stranger but an acquaintance, friend, or relative, in some ways it's even harder. Here the risk is alienating someone you may care about. In making your point, you may lose a valued relationship or be dismissed as scolding or being self-righteous.

I think there are two things you can do here: Talk to Kevin later about the comment. Tell him what you think and why. Don't let it pass without a comment. He needs to know that you don't agree, that you find such remarks unacceptable.

The second thing you can do is open a conversation about bias. Talk about where they come from, the effect they have on people, and so forth. But, once again, refrain from lecturing. There should be a true sharing here—a dialogue, not a monologue.

29.

Give Your Children Books That Show Different Kinds of People Playing, Working, and Living Together

There was a time when children's books presented only one type of American family. It was the *Father Knows Best / Ozzie and Harriet* family. Each family had a father who went to work and a mother who stayed at home with their two children. They lived in a suburban house and rode in a new car along roads without traffic jams. Children who read those books often thought the whole world was like that. If their lives didn't fit the model, then the fault lay with them.

Today, book publishers are rushing to keep up with the changing nature of family life. America has become a multicultural, multiracial, multilingual society in which Chinese restaurants are as common as hamburger stands, and salsa has replaced ketchup as the country's favorite condiment. Nearly one in two children experiences divorce, and it is not unusual to find a child raised by a single parent.

This doesn't necessarily mean that Jennifer will personally know children who are different from her. People still pretty much tend to cluster with those who are like them, share the same tastes, follow the same religion, and so forth. Most children go to school with others who are in the main quite a bit like themselves. It is important to broaden Jennifer's horizons, to give her the chance to appreciate the diversity of life and to respect the differences among people.

One way to give Jennifer what she might otherwise not personally experience is to provide her with books that show her a world in which a variety of people—ordinary people—go about living their lives, finding joys and setbacks, just as she does. The point of this is to show her that there are people who look different but who, in the most basic way, are actually like her. As Shylock says to his tormentors in *The Merchant of Venice*, "If you prick us, do we not bleed? If you tickle us, do we not laugh? If you poison us, do we not die? And if you wrong us, shall we not revenge?"

Kevin and Jennifer may find Shakespeare too difficult. But there are many books suitable for their age and reading level. They aren't hard to find; check your local libraries and bookstores. You just need to seek them out. Some of my favorites for young children are *Peter's Chair*, by Jack Ezra Keats; *Corduroy*, by Don Freeman; *Tar Beach*, by Faith Ringold; and *All the Colors of the Earth*, by Sheila Hamanaka.

30.

Talk About Differences Between People, but Talk About Them Neutrally

You're in a mall with Kevin and an older woman comes by using a walker. He stares at her as she shuffles by, and you are hoping against hope that he won't say anything to embarrass you or her. You want him to accept differences among people, so if he does make a comment, it is tempting to give a little lecture. Worse is for you to pretend that differences don't exist.

I know a woman named Charmagne who is trying to raise her five-year-old son without prejudice. A black woman herself, she wants Sean to accept people regardless of their color or background. She doesn't want him to put people into categories simply on the basis of skin color.

So Charmagne tries hard to create an atmosphere that avoids the prejudices that plague the larger society. She selects books for him that depict characters of all kinds in a positive light, she monitors the television shows he watches, she makes sure that she talks with him about the contributions of many different ethnic and racial groups. Charmagne scrupulously makes sure never to refer to people by their color. She wants Sean to be "color blind."

One day Sean went on a class trip to the zoo.

"Did you like it?" his mother asked him when he returned home.

"Yes," he answered.

"What animal did you like best?"

"The horse," Sean answered immediately.

"Really?" Charmagne said. She then asked what he liked about the horse and he told her.

Wanting to continue to engage him in conversation, she continued, "And what color was the horse?"

Sean replied proudly, "African American."

Charmagne had been so afraid of Sean inheriting society's prejudices that she didn't even want to speak about the color of people. But the fact is that people do come in different shades and our children see these distinctions, as Charmagne soon learned. There is nothing wrong with that. There's no reason why we shouldn't describe someone as the man in the straw hat, the woman with the sandals, the white man standing over there.

The problems arise when the color is used as a way of setting someone apart for no good reason. Why describe the man by his race when referring to him as the one with red suspenders will do? In our society, color is picked out as having particular relevance when, in fact, much of the time it doesn't play a part whatsoever.

Charmagne learned that children see differences, and it is impossible to pretend that they don't exist. Differences often enrich the world. As Chargmagne discovered, it isn't that we should avoid describing people by race. It is part of their physical reality. The important point is that we don't make the differences negative. We can see reality without becoming bigots. We just have to be careful when, how often and why we describe things as we do.

So Kevin refers to the woman using the walker. This is a chance to find out what Kevin thinks about elderly or disabled people. Teachers call this a "teaching moment." Use it to continue your conversation with your son about the important things in life.

Values

Some Values Are More Important Than Others

> His own parents, he that father'd him and she that
> had conceived him in her womb and birth'd him,
> They gave this child more of themselves than that,
> They gave him afterward every day, they became part
> of him.
>
> —WALT WHITMAN, *Leaves of Grass*

You want your children to have good values. That goes without saying. But which values, exactly, do you want them to have? The answer isn't simple. Different people have different values and different cultures have different values. I may value something because it is useful, but you may value something because your grandmother gave it to you. One culture may value ambition and another may value tranquility.

There are also instances in which two people value the same things but for different reasons. There is a story about Igor Stravinsky, one of the twentieth century's leading composers, who was commissioned to write a musical. He refused the offer, insulted by the small fee attached. This same offer was then made to Erik Satie, a well-known French composer. The result was the same. Satie also turned it down, but for a very different reason. He said the offer was too large and big money for art was insulting. In the end, Satie accepted the commission when the fee was lowered to an amount that he considered suitable.

There are also differences in regard to religious values. One religion may prize salvation and another enlightenment. Even within a single religion there can be differences over which values are most important. For example, the Dominican Order founded a university in Paris in 1229 to study theology and to teach the correct doctrine of faith. Two years later, the Franciscans opened their own Parisian university, putting holiness before learning.

When it comes to moral values, there is also a variety of opinions about which are the most important. While Plato and Aristotle contend that wisdom, courage, temperance, and justice are the paramount virtues, Thomas Aquinas believes they are faith, hope, and charity. David Hume placed benevolence at the top of his list. Conversely, the list of vices also vary: ignorance topped the list for Plato and Aristotle, pride for Aquinas, and cruelty for Hume. The highest virtue for Confucius was *jen,* a concept variously translated as "goodness" or "human heartedness." For another Chinese sage, Lao-tzu, the highest virtue is *wei wu wei,* "creative letting-be." For the Hindu, it is doing no harm.

If this weren't confusing enough, most of us are not fully consistent in our own set of values. I know that I'm not. I would like to have everything: I want both love and satisfying work. I want to be generous, emotionally expressive, and honest. But I have limits—limits imposed on me by my biology, by my upbringing, by my environment, by the times in which I live. I have conflicting demands between wanting to say what I feel and not hurting another's feelings, between work obligations and demands of my family. I also have changed directions in my life over time. This last point may reflect a more general disposition of people to change as they age. Psychologist Erik Erikson points out that what we prize and pursue throughout life changes as we mature. At one point we prize friendship most, at another point it is being competent at work, at another it is our spiritual development.

Despite these difficulties, there really is no getting around teaching values to children. You impart them whether you intend to or not. Your actions *and* your words, the things you choose to talk about or ignore, your praise or disapproval, the songs you sing, the games you play, and the stories you read—these convey to your children what you truly prize. Children learn their values, in part, through observation and imitation. This is why role models are important. Parents who refuse to believe this and attempt to be neutral create a vacuum and thereby allow their children to be unduly influenced by other forces instead, such as peers or TV shows.

You need to decide which values you want to impart. If you have been a good moral educator, your children will grow up making their own value choices. They will not be mirror images or carbon copies of you. That is as it should be. Nevertheless, there are basic values—an orientation toward life—that you will pass on. The clearer you can be about what those values are and the more you live by them yourself, the more likely you are to be successful as the moral educators of your children.

Universal Values

You don't need to be completely at sea regarding moral values. You don't have to start all over, as if you were making them up yourself. You can look around to see what philosophers and religious leaders have written. Personally, I find it interesting to look at various cultures to see if there is anything we all agree on. Anthropologists Richard Shweder and Joan Miller from America and Manamohan Mahapatra from Orissa, India, have wondered the same thing. They wanted to know whether moral values are merely cultural products, like pink as a girl's color and blue as a boy's, or whether there were moral values that could be found in widely divergent cultures. They wanted "to identify principles and concepts that might be candidates for moral universals."

The researchers studied three groups of about 250 people each, all composed of equal numbers of males and females. In every group children outnumbered adults about three to one. They questioned middle-class Americans from Chicago and talked to two groups from Bhubaneswar, India, where there were two communities: high-caste Brahmans (keepers of temple rituals, shopkeepers, tailors, property owners, and landlords); and untouchables (agricultural laborers, construction workers, and basket weavers). They were asked questions such as: How serious is the violation? Is it a sin? Would it still be wrong even if no one knew? Would it be best if everyone followed the rule?

Americans and Indians differed considerably in evaluations of the social practices presented. Most Indians believe that it is morally wrong for a widow to eat fish whereas no American finds this objectionable. Most Indians think that it is morally wrong to marry outside one's caste; few Americans thought so. (Is there an American who roots for Romeo and Juliet's parents? Love conquers all, we say. Indians think Westerners strange to marry for love. It is marriage, they say, that creates love, not the other way around.) All the Brahman children between five and seven thought that being beaten by a cane was not only proper but a parental obligation. They thought that physical punishment was a value to be applied to disobedient children everywhere. Only 10 percent of American children understood caning this way. Likewise, 60 percent of the Indian adults believed it to be a universal virtue; 15 percent of the American adults agreed.

The anthropologists found that between the ages of five and seven, children in all three groups agree with most of the virtues and vices that are identified by the adults in their society. In other words, until about seven, children's morality is a reflection of their culture's rules and values.

Where does this leave us in our search for universal values? Here the researchers give us good news. Unlike most other anthropologists, who contend that morality is arbitrarily chosen by each culture, Schweder, Miller, and Mahapatra found that there may well be moral universals. The analysis of their data provides the following conclusion: There are nine virtues and vices found among American children and adults, Brahman adults, and untouchable adults, moral do's and don'ts that are understood by all adults as objective, unalterable, and universally binding. The virtues are keeping promises, respecting private property, fairly allocating rewards and punishments, protecting the vulnerable, and reciprocating with gratitude. The vices are incest, arbitrary assault, nepotism and bias, and biased classification.

The vices and virtues Shweder and co-workers discovered apply to more than just Americans and Indians. I think these anthropologists have, in fact, identified values that cut across all cultures. This isn't to say that everyone agrees with them all or that everyone agrees on how they apply to particular situations. Translating of values into behavior involves judgment. But these virtues and vices get to the basis of what, as a minimum, human beings need to do to live with one another.

Some of the vices are really the converse of the virtues. The prohibition against incest (whatever biologic reasons there may be behind the taboo) is really a rule that protects the most innocent and vulnerable among us. Children can't protect themselves. They need adults for that. The incest taboo functions to keep children safe from those who, if so inclined, can most take advantage of them, namely, the ones on whom they most rely.

Nepotism is the unfair advantage given to some at the expense of others. In other words, it is the violation of the principle of treating people fairly. The prohibition against arbitrary assault is meant both to protect the vulnerable and to ensure that rewards and punishments are commensurate with the behavior of individuals.

Reciprocity is a form of cooperation. It enforces fairness in dealings with one another, and it is a way of fostering exchange between people without the resort to force. Gratitude keeps the social wheels greased.

Respect for private property is found even in the simplest societies. The Maasai lived near my home in Kenya. Up until the 1960s the concept of private ownership was largely foreign to the Maasai. Members of an extended family, perhaps as many as fifty individuals, work together communally, building their houses in a single compound. Women raise children together, boys herd cattle together, and initiation ceremonies involve large numbers of people. Until recently no one owned land. They couldn't conceive of the idea of anyone possessing the earth. Despite this, they did have a sense of private property. It was a spear or blanket that was called one's own. A woman had her own beads and leather skirt. These belonged to a single individual and private ownership was respected.

The values found in America and India fall into two basic categories. One type of value encourages amicable relations by focusing on impartial treatment. This reflects a natural propensity—we all want to be treated fairly. At one time or another, every child has declared, "That's not fair!" This sense of fairness matures over time. Nevertheless, there is an innate sense about this value. When someone feels that this basic precept is violated, he is resentful, angry, withdrawn, or hostile. Violating this sense of justice unravels the social networks we need to rely on as human beings.

The other type of universal value is designed to prevent harm to the vulnerable. This, too, issues from our nature as social creatures who depend on one another for survival. Truth telling and the prevention of gratuitous violence are both types of social insurance. They establish trust; and, as expressed by novelist Sue Helpern, "Trusting each other is the beginning of a certain secular faith, a faith that allows us to live in families and communities and nations."

The two broad categories of values are related to each other because they address basic conditions necessary for human survival. They provide guidelines that, if followed, keep us from isolating ourselves from one another. I am thinking about philosopher John Kekes's definition of evil as "undeserved harm." The reason evil plays a central role for both religious and secular philosophies is that its presence "jeopardizes human aspirations to live good lives." When a person is harmed through no fault of her own we are in the presence of evil. And who is more open to such harm than the weak, the sick, and children?

Heroes and Role Models

Children, from as early as age four, seem to understand that helping someone in trouble (preventing harm to the innocent) is desirable. This desire to help the distressed leads to the consideration of another source of moral education: heroes.

Having heroes is only natural. Everyone—but especially children—needs people to look up to, people whose deeds, values, and principles are worthy of emulation. Young children think in concrete ways, and heroes offer specific examples of admirable behavior. A hero is also a character in a story, and children are more likely to learn moral lessons through narratives than they are through lectures or aphorisms.

Heroes are illustrations of a life worth living. Children imagine themselves as their heroes and live out their deeds, at least in their imaginations. Kevin and Jennifer put themselves in the place of their heroes and in that way test out what it is like to live like the person they admire.

Who Kevin and Jennifer select as their heroes will likely change with time. As they mature, their notions of what and who are heroes will mature, just as their abilities to feel and think do. Typically, young children—say kindergartners and first graders—define a hero as someone who saves people. This is often the age at which children are fascinated with comic book heroes, fictional characters whose superpowers are used in the aid of rescuing others. Heroes for these children possess physical characteristics that make them heroes. When I was a child, my hero was the comic book character Captain Marvel, who, before uttering the magic word *shazam,* was the lame boy Billy Batson.

By the time children are eight or nine years old, they identify heroic attributes with qualities other than physical ones, such as being brave, good, nice, or trustworthy. Typically, children this age focus on only one of these qualities. The definition of heroism remains the same as that of younger children. It still rests mainly on the act of saving someone or something. At this age, my attention switched from comic books to sports. My hero became Jackie Robinson. His exploits on the field seemed heroic to me, carrying the Dodgers to victory on his own shoulders. It didn't hurt that I lived in Brooklyn.

Things begin to shift more decisively by the time children are eleven to thirteen years old. Now a hero becomes someone to look up to. What makes someone a hero can be either a particular act performed, such as rescuing someone from a burning building, or a more general way of being, such as having done good things for others. In a study of children's conceptions of heroes, Stephen White and Joseph O'Brien quote one fifteen-year-old they interviewed as saying, "a hero to me is someone who goes beyond the call of duty to do good, someone with good morals, someone you can look up to." By the seventh grade, I had become interested in American history. Now my hero was Robert E. Lee. Something about him seemed dignified. It wasn't his defense of the Confederacy that attracted me but his nobility even in loss. He seemed the reluctant soldier, a model of a good officer.

The notion of heroes becomes more complex for children older than fifteen. A hero becomes harder to define for this age group. However, a new consideration seems to be added to the mix, and that is the hero's beliefs and motivations and the consequences of their actions. So a late adolescent may say something like, "a hero is someone who stands up for his beliefs, regardless of consequences." If you think back to the work of Kohlberg, you can see how this last view of heroes fits with stage 5 thinking. This is the stage known as the golden rule, at which the values of justice and liberty become universal and upheld regardless of majority opinion.

One of the interesting points in examining children's heroes is that, with the exception of five- and six-year-olds, who focus a lot on cartoon characters, those most likely to be identified as heroes were parents, other family members, and friends. Again, this shouldn't be surprising because the earlier stages of moral thinking focus on small groups, especially personal relations. Children think in terms of the people they know, the people with whom they interact. Of course, some children name sports figures, entertainers, and so forth, but at no point do they constitute the majority.

As children mature, they move away from responses such as, "My mom is my hero because when I get into trouble, she helps me," or "My father is my hero because I love him." An older student wrote that his father was his hero because he "sold his business, left the town where he lived for forty-five years, to move here for my brother and me."

Moral Identity

Values are only as good as the behavior they lead to. To value success but not work hard at succeeding is empty rhetoric. It is the same with moral values. It's not enough that your child says, "It's wrong that some students pick on others." It is important that she does something about it. William Damon, the director of the Center on Adolescence at Stanford University, and Ann Colby of the Carnegie Foundation find that most people believe that it is wrong to allow others to suffer but only a small percentage conclude that they themselves must do something about it. What was the difference between the two groups? Damon

and Colby write that people who thought they had to take action were those whose

> concerns about human suffering are central to the way
> they think about themselves and their life goals, and so
> they feel a responsibility to take action, even at great
> personal cost. . . . People who define themselves in terms
> of their moral goals are likely to see moral problems in
> everyday events, and they are also likely to see themselves
> as necessarily implicated in these problems.

The difference between those who take action and those who
don't isn't necessarily the difference in the ability to feel or reason about moral matters. And it may not be a matter of self-
esteem or courage. The difference may turn on what Damon
calls "moral identity." When a person's self-image coincides
with moral concerns, she is likely to be moved to action. Moral
identity begins to take shape in late childhood. Until then, children typically identify themselves in terms of specific, measur-
able traits or interests. They say they are good at math or a
good dancer or funny. Only with the onset of adolescence do
they begin to identify themselves in moral terms, such as, "I'm
kind," or "I'm a fair person."

Whether your children develop moral identities or not depends, in part, on you. If your primary values are moral values,
then the chances are that this will also be true of your children.
Moral identity hinges on a number of influences in their lives,
but the values you espouse and the kind of life you lead convey
strong messages. As Damon writes, "For most children, parents
are the original source of moral guidance."

31.

Tell Your Children About the People You Admire and Why

Like most children, Kevin and Jennifer probably have heroes. There are comic book heroes, television and movie heroes, and sports heroes. There are historical and contemporary figures, and mythic and fictional characters that become models in your children's eyes.

Some of the heroes truly present admirable qualities, but others are of a more questionable nature. Some athletes show good sportsmanship; others are bullies. Some entertainers contribute to charities; others merely indulge themselves.

The entertainment industry, the purpose of which isn't moral edification but, rather, to sell us something, is the prime mover behind which people or characters are presented to us for consideration. Even political figures come packaged as products, not given to us as personalities with principles.

Chances are that your child has a moral hero. If you asked her to name one, she may well name you. Most children really do admire their parents; they want to be like them.

So it is important for you to offer them some indirect guidance in terms of ethical values by letting them know whom you admire. That way they learn from you what attributes you think constitute an ethical person.

You can build on the esteem they hold for you by letting them know about the people who have influenced your moral life. The writer Chaim Potok once said, "Through our heroes we announce to one another who and what we really are." So our children will know more about us as we let them know whom we hold in high regard.

Today one of my heroes is Aung San Suu Kyi, the winner of the Nobel Prize for peace from Myanmar Burma. She spent many years under house arrest after she won a democratically held election but was denied taking office by the military dictatorship. Not only does she exhibit extraordinary physical courage but she is modest, kind, and thoughtful. I think how much better everyone would be if people like her chose public office.

As an adult, I've also learned that ordinary people leading ordinary lives can be heroes. These are the little heroes, people who because of their actions day after day, make all the difference. Several years ago I heard about the residents of North Platte, Nebraska, who every day for three years, during World War II, met trains filled with soldiers on their way to war. These housewives and farmers, merchants and schoolchildren brought doughnuts and coffee for the troops. They sat with the young men and women, giving them encouragement and support, as they went to their uncertain fate.

For me, the people of North Platte are also heroes, not the kind who set records or have their names lit up on the movie marquee or are recorded in history books. They are the little heroes, whose names are forgotten in history but who, in the long run, make all the difference.

32.

Live Your Life As You Want Your Children to Lead Theirs

By the time your children reach adolescence, they know what you believe and the ethical principles you hold dear. Actions speak louder than words, is the adage. Our children know a great deal about what we think and what we value just by watching us. They have lived with us long enough to know more than we can tell them.

Despite this, there is an unfortunate temptation to preach. If we just say something loudly and forcefully enough, it will penetrate. Although there is good reason to express our outrage over something that is especially disturbing, the fact is that preaching has little effect. Telling Jennifer how to live her life isn't anywhere as effective as living your life the way you want Jennifer to live hers. Real-life examples—your life, in particular—are more important than the most eloquent sermons or carefully crafted lessons.

Writers are told to show, not tell. The same can be said to parents. It is not what you tell Kevin that matters, it is what you show him that counts.

The trick here is not so different from being a good leader. There is a story about Dwight Eisenhower that makes the point about effective leadership. He placed a piece of string on the table and asked his pupil to pull it. Eisenhower then straightened the string and asked the person to push it.

"You see," he said, "pull the string, and it will follow you wherever you wish. Push it and it will go nowhere at all."

Rabbi Wayne Dosick, in his book *Golden Rules*, tells this

story about Mohandas Gandhi. Gandhi was viewed by many not only as a political leader but also as a wise man who could be consulted about all sorts of problems, moral, and otherwise. One day a distraught mother brought her son to see him.

"I'm very concerned about my son," she explained. "I'm afraid that he is eating sugar and it isn't good for him."

"But why bring him to me?" Gandhi asked. "I know little about such things. Besides, I'm not a doctor."

"Yes. But he respects you," she said. "So I know he will listen to you."

Gandhi agreed to meet with the boy. They talked about many things, but he said nothing about the sugar. Finally, Gandhi told the boy to come back in two weeks.

Two weeks later they met again. They still didn't discuss the boy's eating habits. After a while he told him to return in two weeks. When the boy returned for the third time, Gandhi asked him to please stop eating sugar.

Later the mother reported that the boy had indeed stopped eating sugar. But, she wanted to know, why did he send him away and simply not tell him what to do the first time he saw him.

"Because first I had to stop eating sugar myself," Gandhi explained.

33.

Show the Importance of Protecting
the Vulnerable

Linnie's story is a good example of a concerned thirteen-year-old. She lived in a weatlhy village on Long Island with her mother, Mary Ann, a woman who commuted to New York during the workweek.

One Saturday Mary Ann decided to take Linnie to Manhattan to spend the day visiting museums. By midday they stopped at a coffee shop for lunch. Linnie ordered a sandwich, but ate only half.

Mary Ann gently encouraged her to finish it, but Linnie wouldn't hear of it.

When it was time to leave, Linnie surprised her mother by asking the waitress to wrap the leftover part of the sandwich so she could take it with her. "At least she will eat it later," Mary Ann thought. "It won't go to waste."

As they were ready to leave, Linnie asked the waitress to give her a covered cup of water and napkins.

"Wait a minute, Mom," she said when they were outside.

She then walked to a disheveled, bearded man who was sitting on the sidewalk next to a shopping cart full of empty cans and discarded things.

She handed him her sandwich.

"I saw him when we came in to eat," she said to her mother when she returned. "I wanted him to have something to eat, too, so I saved half my sandwich for him."

Where did Linnie get her idea from? Her offering half her sandwich to a stranger, in fact, came from witnessing expressions of sympathy and concern within her family. Her mother works for an organization for blind people. Linnie grew up with a woman who had devoted her professional life to working with people with special needs. Linnie's mother modeled caring qualities by the very career she had chosen.

Although most adults are not in the helping professions, there are still many ways in which children learn from what parents do. They may see volunteer work in the community; they overhear conversations in which we express our feelings about the less fortunate. We may shop for a sick neighbor or contribute to a charity. Often something as simple as demonstrating politeness in everyday situations leaves an indelible mark on the child. We also teach by the way we react to harm shown in a movie or to an accident reported on the news. We teach empathy by calling attention to the emotional lives of others. If our child hurts another, we talk about the way this has made the other person feel. If our child is suffering, we extend our sympathy to him. Families that raise empathetic children are often families that talk about feelings.

Mary Anne praised Linnie's thoughtfulness, thereby rewarding Linnie's considerateness.

34.

Comment on Compassionate Behavior—Let Your Children Know That Caring Is an Important Value

Kevin and Jennifer will know a great deal about what you value without your saying a word. They will know because they have lived with you and have seen what you do and what you value. They will have observed your lives and from that they will understand what you think is important.

Still, it doesn't hurt to reinforce your values by relating stories or anecdotes that reflect your ethical sense. Your children will hear much from others who value things other than ethics—success, sexual allure, material possessions. Your verbal reassurances will serve as ballast against the more crass and commercial values that saturate our lives.

Compassion—caring about others—gets short shrift in the media. But occasionally there will be a story about someone who has done something selflessly for others. There are people who volunteer for the fire department or give money to a good cause. When you hear about such people, you can bring them into your conversation.

A wonderful story that exemplifies compassion appeared in newspapers and TV shows around the country several years ago. It was a story that offered the opportunity to comment on the kindness that people can show one another. Joshua Jordan, a fifth grader, had undergone treatment for childhood leukemia. But he was determined to stay in school despite the difficulty of his treatment and the fact that he lost all his hair. His school principal, Paul Swem, held a classroom meeting to ask how the students might be able to help Joshua. Many suggestions were made that day but one captured everyone's imagination. The children decided to have their heads shaved so Joshua wouldn't feel awkward or alone. The idea spread beyond Joshua's classroom, until the entire school was behind the idea. One day, twenty-one children from first grade to fifth, two teachers, and two fathers in front of a cheering student and parent gathering got buzz cuts.

There's no reason to be silent about the things that matter to you. The voice of a parent is often the voice of conscience that is heard as an adult. And it is better that the voice heard is the one saying, "This is the right thing to do," than one that is full of fear, guilt, or shame.

35.

*Let Your Children Know What You Value
and Why You Value It*

You and your children may well disagree about certain things. Kevin may argue with you about how telling the teacher that the dog ate his homework is no big deal. Children are inventive in justifying what they want. Sometimes it isn't easy to distinguish novel approaches from rationalizing bad behavior. Young children have a hard time distinguishing between telling the truth and making up the truth to suit their own needs. The line between the real world and the fantasy world isn't always that distinct in the mind of a four-year-old.

As children mature, they develop their own likes and dislikes and have strong thoughts about what is important or not. Jennifer will have her own set of values. It is important to keep in mind that not all values are equal. While we want to respect our children's individuality, not everything they value is right. And if we believe that moral values are more important than other values, we have to make sure that we convey this to them.

Mostly our children will learn about our values by watching what we do. But we'll be of greater help to them if we can be more explicit. I once wrote a code of ethics for adults. Its language is poetic and abstract, really too difficult for children to grasp. Sharon, a Sunday school teacher, took the code and, with her class, rewrote it into a language that young children can understand. Here it is, as rewritten by children ages seven to ten:

People are more important than things.

Don't put others down to make yourself feel good.

Life is special. Treat it with respect.

Everyone's job is important.

Invite guests and travelers into your home.

Your dreams may all come true.

Always be able to say, "I'm sorry."

Never put yourself down.

Never think you are better than someone else.

You can do the same for your own family. Make a list of your own values, talk to your children about them, and together compile your own family's values list.

Here is my code of ethics as I originally prepared it:

Do no harm to the earth, she is your mother.

Being is more important than having.

Never promote yourself at another's expense.

Hold life sacred; treat it with reverence.

Allow each person the dignity of her or his labor.

Open your home to wayfarers.

Be ready to receive your deepest dreams; sometimes they are the speech of unblighted conscience.

Always make restitution to the ones you have harmed.

Never think less of yourself than you are.

Never think that you are more important than another.

Community

Morality Is Social

Anywhere is the center of the earth.
— BLACK ELK, in *Black Elk Speaks*

You have done everything you can to raise a moral child. You have helped him understand his own and others' feelings, cultivated independent thinking, and been a good role model. By and large, you have been consistent and authoritative as a parent and have steered clear of using fear, guilt, or shame to control his behavior. What more is there to say, then, about helping your child on the road to becoming an ethical person?

Most of what I've talked about up to now has been about your relationship to your child. But there is more to it than that. Although you as a parent play a pivotal role in your child's moral development, you are only one of several factors that influence your children. They have peers, go to school, belong to organizations, watch television, and may have a computer on which they play video games or are hooked up to the Internet. They also live in a world affected by politics, economics, and cultural attitudes. All this is part of the atmosphere in which they grow and develop their moral sensibilities.

In this last section, then, I want to shift the focus away from you and on to society as a whole. This isn't to diminish your responsibility but rather to put it into its proper setting. The fact is that no matter how well intentioned or motivated you may be, you can use some help. Or to put it another way, the society in which a person lives either helps or hinders our children's moral development.

For thousands of years, people have recognized that humans are social creatures. An anecdote about Confucius illustrates the point. A duke once asked Confucius what to do about crime in his domain. For thirteen years Confucius traveled from state to state, visiting jails, attempting to find out what the prisoners had in common. He returned to his patron's court to report on his findings. Confucius said that if the duke wanted to put a stop to crime, he needed to do two things: Teach everyone how to read, and find work for every man. Illiteracy and unemployment were the main causes of crime, he said, not lack of discipline or too little love.

About two hundred years later and half a world away Aristotle also made the connection between morality and social structures. Aristotle, like Confucius, viewed humans as social creatures and as such subject to the social structures in their society. Good societies make for good people, Aristotle said, because society came before the individual. What he meant was that we are always born into an already existing situation. Those raised in a democracy will have one set of values. Those raised under tyranny will have another. No one is self-made or starts from nowhere. We speak the language with which we were raised, we eat what others around us eat, and we start by believing what others teach us is right.

Moral education, whether in the classroom, at home, or in the community, is effective to the extent to which the various components work to support one another. David Blankenhorn, the president of the Institute for American Values, proposes that "a primary goal of public policy and private initiative in the coming generations should be to protect and strengthen civil society." He continues, "Regarding any public policy proposal, the first question to ask should be: Will this policy strengthen or weaken the institutions of civil society?" This is recognition that economic and political decisions by government and business have consequences for the lives of families. Families no more live in isolation from society than children do from adults. Recently, the German government implemented regulations in line with Blankenhorn's recommendations. All legislation considered by the federal government must include a statement regarding the effect such legislation will have on children.

School

Unless Kevin and Jennifer are being home schooled, beginning at about age five and continuing until they are well into their teens they will spend more time with teachers and other students than they will with you. School will increasingly become their major social environment.

Whether they accept the responsibility or not, schools are a major contributor to your child's moral education. How is your child's school doing? If her school falls short in academics, you can always get her a tutor. And if you want her to excel in music, you can arrange private lessons. Is it the same with moral education?

Not exactly. Although moral guidance isn't on the curriculum in most schools, your children will be getting a moral education there all the same. The atmosphere of the school is part of moral education: whether teachers exercise their power fairly or arbitrarily, whether the administrators respect the teachers and custodians, whether intimidation and violence are stopped. Every institutional arrangement implies a moral perspective (top-down vs. egalitarian, for example), and every classroom also contains a set of moral values (the learner as an active person or a passive recipient, as another example). Some have called this the "invisible curriculum." Teaching by example is critical in moral education.

Although parents and educators agree that schools should teach honesty, respect, and responsibility, in fact different values tend to dominate our school systems: academic standards and athletics. The difficulty is that character education requires cooperation, whereas academic standards and sports rely mainly on competition. But doesn't competition make for good character? That is the rationale for the grading system and supporting school sports. Psychologists Elliot Aronson and co-workers have found that in elementary-school classrooms where children work cooperatively to solve problems the level of empathy increases dramatically compared to more traditional classrooms that rely on competition for grades and teachers' attention. The researchers note that in competitive situations, children attribute others' failures to lack of ability and their rival's success to luck. At the same time, they extend the benefit of the doubt to their own failures. They say, "I wasn't feeling well" or "The question wasn't fair."

However, in a cooperative classroom, students extend the same benefit of the doubt to their classmates. They were able to be as generous with the other pupils as they were with themselves. By making students partners rather than competitors, pupils were better able to put themselves emotionally in another's place.

In many schools, because they are built on a competition in which only one person winds up with the accolades, children experience frustration on a regular basis. There are teachers who believe that struggle is desirable. And it is, in small measure. But for many, the goals set are so high that Kevin never succeeds. Rather than being rewarded for his efforts, he is defeated. Goals need to be attainable, then new goals are set. The importance of this insight for moral development is that children who are regularly frustrated will develop stronger prejudices against groups they don't like. This has nothing to do with the behavior of the other group. It is really scapegoating.

So if your children are expressing prejudices against others, you may want to look at what is happening at school and how it is organized. A change in their environment may well change their attitude.

Work

Your children need the steadying influence of a solid family. They require a certain sense of security to thrive. And so do you. If you work in a company that doesn't support your family life, it is difficult to raise your children the way you would like. Unlike many European countries that are generous with allowing employees to be with their families, America is just beginning to recognize that if we value families, then society has to make it easier, not harder, for parents to be with their children. Yet there are few companies that allow for flex hours or provide on-site daycare centers.

In addition, there is a trend toward valuing work over leisure. Even people who are not working are working at something. Everyone is busy, busy, busy. It's un-American to have leisure time, time with nothing to do, time for relaxation, meditation, or reflection. Cellular phones are used in restaurants, parks, and beaches. Hotels have phones in the bathrooms. Children take dancing lessons, have chess club meetings, birthday parties, and sleep-over dates. Everyone is always squeezing things in.

In a *New Yorker* cartoon a woman holds a briefcase and is talking on a cell phone. She is saying, "Don't you dare put Mommy on hold again."

In all this, children get short shrift. It is hard for them to get undivided attention. They have learned not to bother you when you're busy. The problem is you're nearly always busy with something. Being aware of the problem is the first step toward a solution.

Work also takes its toll on families in another way. For the sake of better pay and promotions, families are uprooted. Occasionally, a move takes the family no farther than a mile or two but more often than not it means starting over again. Friends are lost. There is a new school to get used to, a new crowd to become part of, and new organizations to join. Although children will make new friends, the process is unsettling.

In addition, a move *to* somewhere is also a move *away* from someone. Left behind are aunts and uncles, grandparents, and cousins. This puts a strain not only on your children but also on you. No matter how loving a parent, there are limits to one's time and patience. Having relatives nearby helps relieve the pressure. You may well be cross with your child not because she has done anything bad but because you have had a bad day. Having someone to care for your children for even a short while—and someone who deeply cares about them—is a blessing for everyone.

Television and Computers

Consider the following scenario:

The doorbell rings.

"Could you get that, please?" you call to Jennifer.

She opens the door.

"Hello," a well-dressed stranger says. "Do you mind if I come in for a moment?" Before you have a chance to get to the door yourself, you find the man has entered the living room, and he is sitting on the couch. Kevin and Jennifer are listening to him talk, sing, tell jokes, dance, and do magic tricks.

But this stranger isn't all fun. He also sells toys, candy, and beer, talks about sex and exhibits various forms of violence.

You'd be horrified at this unlikely scenario, of course. Well, this is more or less what happens when your children watch television. Strangers occupy the house and engage your children. Commercial media aren't interested in the moral well-being of your children. They want to make a profit; that means selling advertising space. And advertisers aren't interested in the ethical health of your children; they want only to sell their products.

Part of the problem is the content of television programming. There is good reason to be upset by what children watch, day after day, year after year. According to the Kaiser Family Foundation, the average two- to four-year-old watches more than two hours of television a day, and the average eight- to thirteen-year-old watches nearly four hours a day. The American Academy of Pediatrics reports by the age of eighteen, the average young person will have viewed as many as two hundred thousand acts of violence on television. They also report that during the course of one year, the American teenager sees an estimated 14,000 sexual references and innuendoes on television. Only 150 of these deal with sexual responsibility.

The constant exposure to violence and antisocial behavior is a serious problem. Innumerable studies have demonstrated that media violence leads to aggressive behavior in some children. Given the nature of many shows—the graphic nature of news shows with the emphasis on the visually engaging fires, accidents, crime, and war and the commercial nature of the medium—I am astounded that some parents allow their children to watch television unsupervised. I wonder what parent would permit an uninvited stranger into her home to speak to her child alone for an hour. But this is what happens when the TV is turned on.

It is tempting to use television as a form of entertainment. In small doses, there is nothing wrong with that. What's more, watching TV with your child also helps. Robert Kubey and Mihaly Csikszentmihalyi note that discussions about TV shows watched together offer the opportunity for children to share common experiences with their families. "Viewing with the family is clearly a more positive experience than viewing alone," they write. "When television is viewed with family members, it is a significantly more challenging, cheerful, and sociable experience than when viewed alone." The researchers caution, though, that whatever the content of a show, there is a general negative trend associated with television watching, even when viewed with others. Television watching, as a rule, makes people passive and less alert and causes difficulty in concentration.

The problem with television goes beyond the content of the shows. It almost doesn't matter what is on TV; it's that the TV

is on that matters. The sheer number of hours children spend
in front of the screen (whether it's TV or the computer) is in
itself a problem. Moral development depends on children inter-
acting with others. It is through the experience of encountering
the desires of others that children learn how to behave in acceptable ways to accommodate the legitimate needs of all.

Religion and Morality

Throughout the country, fewer and fewer parents are participating in parent-teacher organizations. Several of my elementary-
school teacher friends, from poor districts to affluent ones, tell
me that they have little or no contact with most of their pupils'
parents. They send notes home fully aware that they are likely to
go unread.

On the whole, church membership is in decline, as is attendance at worship services. So what are people doing instead?
Aside from television watching and playing with the computer,
they're going to the mall, or at least it seems to me that way.
However, shopping is not the same kind of communal activity
as is league bowling or PTA meetings. Although done in the
presence of others, walking, browsing, and hanging out in the
mall is based on a consumer ethic, not a civic one. A shopping
plaza is a private space, governed not by public policy but by
private gain. Spending time with someone in the mall is akin to
what toddlers do in nursery school—play side by side but not
with each other.

For a variety of complex reasons, Americans are not as engaged in social activities as they once were. The camaraderie
that comes from being part of a common effort is absent when
activities are pursued alone. This is especially serious for the
development of the moral sensibilities of children. They are deprived of real-life encounters in which real people have real
feelings. Just as significant is the necessity of learning to be tol-

erant of different opinions, being part of a group effort, and developing the art of compromise.

In response to the breakdown in community life, churches and schools are once again being called on to play a role in character education. I once appeared on a television show with an evangelical preacher and a conservative politician. We were discussing a ruling by a school district that had barred religious clubs from meeting on school premises (a position that all three of us thought wrong). The conversation turned to the morality of children, and both the minister and the politician were certain that they could pinpoint the time in which America's morals went into decline. "The day the Supreme Court took prayers out of the schools," they insisted. They, like other parents who are concerned about moral education, believe that without religious guidance and instruction, without a belief in God, morality is impossible. The evidence to support this claim, however, is far from certain. Sociologist Robert Wuthnow reviewed the scholarly and popular literature to see if there is a relationship between participation in religious organizations and charitable behavior. He writes, "There is some evidence that religious participation encourages people to become involved in activities that actually benefit the needy. The kinds of activities that are encouraged seem to be ones closely connected with the church itself." Wuthnow concludes:

What the evidence on religious participation suggests is that churchgoing does not seem to generate convictions about caring that carry over into all realms of the believer's life. People do not, for example, see caring acted out in their churches and then go out with such conviction about the importance of caring that they help the next person they see. Instead, what they see and hear in church channels their caring. It is channeled, above all, into programs the church as an organization is trying to promote. After this it is channeled informally among members and into certain kinds of traditionally accepted behaviors. One's definition of what constitutes a need and, when it is appropriate to care is, in short, shaped by the organization one attends.

While Wuthnow looked at the relationship between caring and religion, others have looked at the relationship between religion and crime. The conclusion is that neither the intensity of religious beliefs nor the degree to which one believes in divine rewards and punishments inhibited criminality. However, the more frequent the attendance at religious services or study groups, the lower the crime rate. Byron Johnson of Lamar University in Texas also found a relationship between religion and the rehabilitation of prisoners. In his study, Lamar found that inmates who participated significantly in prison fellowship programs were less likely to be rearrested than prisoners with low or medium participation rates. What is unclear from the research is whether it is religion per se that makes the difference or whether it is participation in a group dedicated to prosocial values that helps keep people from committing crimes or former prisoners from reverting to their old patterns of antisocial behavior. When a person is engaged in religious activities, she is entangled with other people. The association itself may be the strongest positive influence on her behavior, not the religious factor.

The research regarding the relationship between religion and caring echoes that found by the Oliners and by Fogelman. For some Germans, religious convictions led them to altruistic acts. For others, however, religion didn't lead to helping Jews or prevent them from being bystanders. At the same time, there were Holocaust rescuers who weren't religious at all. They were motivated by ethical principles or by their moral identity, which wouldn't allow them to live with themselves if they did nothing in the face of evil.

These conclusions are consistent with the findings of educational psychologist Larry Nucci. He found that children's moral understanding is independent of their understanding of religious requirements. Nucci notes that "children's conceptions of morality cannot be accounted for in terms of a simple adherence to God's word. Instead children attempt to coordinate their notions of God with what they *know to be morally right*" (emphasis in the original). So, for example, when children were asked if God could command something bad to be good, most children rejected the idea. God could require people to do only good things. In other words, certain deeds weren't good because God commanded a person to do them. Rather, God made such commandments because the actions were already good.

The research suggests that religion may play a supporting, although not primary, role for some people in creating ethical behavior. In the main, moral behavior and religious commitment have little relation to one another. Whether someone is a believer or atheist is no predictor of altruistic or reprehensible behavior.

Market Values and Moral Values

Moral values aren't the only values we hold. Many people also value success. It is hard to instill moral values when other values are taken more seriously, given more weight, and are reinforced daily by many segments of society. As explained by political science professor Andrew Hacker, America "poises its citizens against one another, with the warning that they must make it on their own. Hence the stress on moving past others, driven by a fear of falling behind. No other nation so rates its residents as winners or losers."

The desire to succeed all too often means succeeding at any cost. In many communities, having winning teams is not only more important than academic achievement but also more important than ethics. Teachers, administrators, and communities indulge successful athletes and overlook immoral behavior and even criminal behavior—as long as the athlete or team is successful. A championship trumps honest play. Schools are reluctant to discipline top athletes because the team may lose the next game and thereby the prestige and money that come along with winning. Professional athletes garner commercial endorsements as long as they are at the top of their game. And parents push their children to succeed, at any cost to ethical values, because of the vicarious thrill it gives them. "The sad truth is," writes *Newsday* sports columnist Harvey Araton, "monuments and trophy cases are built faster for jocks who score than for champions of virtue."

Another reason for the failure to create character-forming institutions is financial. Good schools, daycare, and recreation centers and safe, suitable playgrounds aren't cheap. Among the twenty wealthiest countries, the United States ranked last in social spending on its young and ranked next to last on spending on education. In other words, America isn't willing to pay the cost of reviving the institutions that make a difference in forming moral character. Congress, faced with a surplus in the federal budget in 1999, chose a tax refund to an investment in the future of American families.

Family therapist Mary Pipher, who is concerned about the cultural forces that are pulling families apart, presents several strategies to challenge the prevailing norms in society. One of her suggestions is that parents create spaces in their neighborhoods where people of all ages can gather for common experiences. This idea goes against the grain in our society where we segregate people according to age, race, and class. Her suggestion is consistent with findings in the area of moral psychology that understanding someone else's point of view is part of the underpinnings of character building. Pipher also urges families to participate in the national TV-free week in April and, throughout the year, to find games and activities to do together. She could easily have agreed with the slogan common on streets in Serbia in 1996, "Switch off the TV; switch on your mind." "One person can make a difference," Pipher writes. "People . . . needn't feel that they must change the world single-handedly. . . . Just because a person can't do everything doesn't mean he/she should do nothing."

In addition to individual efforts made at moral education, people who raise children must live in a society that supports such efforts. There is little disagreement about the desirability of parents taking responsibility for raising moral children. However, parents can't stand alone and expect to be particularly successful. This isn't a liberal or conservative position but one that is self-evident. Simply stated: There are conditions under which people are inclined to be virtuous. We know what those conditions are—safety and stability, steady work, and good education. The great debate in our society today is how to achieve such conditions. Raising a moral child requires efforts not only by the family but by all of society as well. Families are best supported by a society that cares for the adults who, in turn, are then best able to raise moral children.

The Larger Community

Your children live in ever-widening circles, from the immediate family to the human family, from the neighborhood to the globe. What happens has an effect on them, even if they never leave home. The lives of all human beings are increasingly related, because there no longer is anywhere that is remote or untouched. What happens far away has an effect on Kevin and Jennifer right here.

Mathematicians and other scientists have poetically termed this the butterfly effect. They use the example of the flight of a butterfly in China and how the beating of its wings one day will influence the weather in Boston the next week. This is just as true in the social world, in the realms of economics and politics, for example. Just think how the gyrations of the financial markets in Japan, Europe, and Brazil affect the economic well-being of people in Wyoming and British Columbia. And think about how the cutting of the Amazon rain forest is changing the environment in Chicago.

Knowing this as a general rule doesn't outline specific things to do. We don't know exactly how any one thing affects anything else. There are too many factors involved. Not only is there a butterfly in China but there are also sparrows in Los Angeles and moving oxcarts in India. This is why the formal name for this theory is chaos theory.

Despite the impossibility of accurately predicting the way far-off events affect things local, the basic point isn't in dispute: Everything in the world is tied together in some way; what happens one place has some influence on events even at the most distant point.

Wayne Dosick, in his book *Golden Rules: The Ten Ethical Values Parents Need to Teach Their Children*, expresses the same idea in this story:

> A farmer, whose corn always took first prize at the state fair, always shared his best corn seeds with all the neighboring farmers.
>
> When asked why, he said, "The wind picks up the pollen, and carries it from field to field. If my neighbors grow poor corn, the cross-pollination will bring down the quality of my corn. But, if they plant the very best seeds, then their corn and my corn will always be the most excellent quality. What is good for my neighbors is good for me.

We know that there are certain institutional conditions that make it easy to be virtuous and that when those conditions are absent, it is difficult—but not impossible—for people to act ethically. We know that those conditions are safety, stability, and education. This much is beyond dispute. What isn't clear is how to achieve such conditions for all children and families. When the institutional conditions are in place, the psychological conditions for an ethical life are easier to achieve.

36.

Supervise Your Children's Television Viewing

You wouldn't let your children use a power saw without your supervision, nor do you keep prescription drugs around the house without safety caps on. There's no reason to treat TV any differently. It is an enormously powerful tool and as such needs to be treated carefully.

TV isn't going to disappear. But you can take steps to keep it in check. The most radical step you can take is to not have a TV in your house. The American Academy of Pediatrics recommends that children under two not watch any television at all. There are families who have chosen to forgo the set for the sake of other pleasures. They may simply be together, one reading, one doing a crossword puzzle, one cooking. You may not want to go so far, but it is worth trying out. Instead, declare one day a week without television. Your children will protest, but if you are convinced that TV is deleterious to your children's moral development, you may insist on the experiment. See what happens. You have as much right to insist on this, if you choose, as you do forbidding certain foods to your children because you believe they are unhealthy.

Some homes choose to limit the number of hours per week that children are permitted to watch TV. You can then decide whether they are free to choose whatever they want to watch or whether you will limit this for them, too. The V-chip now available makes this easier to monitor. (A similar device is available for the Internet, barring particular Web sites from use.)

Use television sparingly as a baby-sitter. The problem with TV watching is that it becomes a substitute for human interaction. Children need to be involved with others to receive the stimulation necessary for ethical growth.

Keep the television as family property, not an individual possession. This is also a recommendation of the American Academy of Pediatrics. They suggest that children's rooms be "electronic media free zones." Once your child has a TV in her own room, you won't be able to supervise what she sees, you won't be able to talk about it, and you won't be able to interact in a meaningful way. Negotiating what shows to watch can be a useful exercise in cooperation.

Watch television together, if possible. Even if you hate wrestling, spend at least a few minutes with Jennifer if this is her favorite show. Maybe you can understand her better or perhaps she may learn to appreciate why you don't like it. Respectful dialogue is important. This can happen, even around television.

37.

Get Involved with Your Children's Education

All schools teach morality. There's no way around it. There may be classes in character education, moral development, or values clarification. But, in fact, such classes are the least of it. What your child really learns about ethics and values isn't found in the school catalog. Real moral lessons are found everywhere—in the library, in the classroom, in the cafeteria, and in the teachers' and administrators' offices. Every place people meet one another, that is where ethics are taught. It is the general atmosphere of the school, the nature of the relationships of all whom occupy the school building, that provides the real moral education.

Attend school games, go to school plays. See the way students are treated. Observe the attitude of the coach or director. Is sportsmanship more important than winning? Are athletes encouraged to respect their opponents or the opposite? How much does the school spend on athletics compared to compensatory classes for the least-able student?

Follow contract negotiations in the school district. Are teachers paid fairly? Is bargaining done in good faith? Does the well-being of the student remain foremost?

Many institutions make decisions based on what's good for the institution. Does the school feel more like a factory or a home? Are rules and regulations aimed at making the school a place of real learning or are they aimed mainly at orderliness and control? To what extent does the school treat students as people rather than impediments to smooth functioning?

Students respect school authority if they believe that teachers' and administrators' actions are fair. Even the youngest students are concerned about fairness and human welfare. When a teacher (or school system) is viewed as unfair and biased, then whatever is said about moral behavior falls on deaf ears. So observe the way in which rules are enforced. Don't expect special treatment for your child, but also be concerned if other children aren't treated fairly.

If the school says one thing but does another, call the administrators, teachers, and school board to task. Ultimately, you are responsible for providing your children with a sound moral education. Don't let a school squander your good efforts at home.

Finally, take a hard look at the school and measure how they are doing against these three factors: Do the teachers and administrators care about the individual student, are the teachers and administrators truthful, and do the teachers and administrators try to solve conflicts fairly?

38.

Make Family Meals Important and Regular Occasions

There is something about sitting together to eat that cannot be replaced. "Breaking bread together" is a universal symbol of friendship, community, and communion. Wherever you go, strangers are welcomed by being given something to eat and drink, whether crackers and soda, wine and cheese, or whatever the local custom.

Eating is so basic that those things done while eating also become embedded in our beings. The slogan "The family that prays together stays together" has validity. Prayers said around the dinner table reinforce the bonds between family members and the wider world around them. The equivalent of prayers is available to the more secularly minded. You can begin each meal by reading a favorite quote of yours, a different one for each day of the year. The quotes should express an ethical or spiritual aspiration of yours, and they can range from the sublime to the ridiculous.

Many of the quotes you read may make little sense to your children when they are young. But as they get older, they begin to grasp the meaning. Even if they don't remember the quotes, the very act of being together means a great deal. It is a place where they feel welcome, secure, important, respected, and wanted.

The very structure and repetition of meals creates a family ritual. Being able to count on the same thing day after day helps reduce anxiety. And as you know, an anxious person has a difficult time being an ethical person.

So make sure you make the opportunity to sit together, eat together, and talk together. What you do and say around mealtime with older children will have a greater impact than doing and saying similar things at any other time.

39.
- - - - - - - - - -

Make Time for Your Children

Keep a log of all your waking hours over the course of a month. This may seem time-consuming, but people who keep such a detailed account are often astonished by the discrepancy between how they thought they spent their time and what they actually did. Workers find that they thought they were working hard on one task only to find that in reality they spent more on another.

A log will tell you how much time you spend with your children, whether in person or through some other means. Ask yourself whether this is sufficient or whether there is another way to allocate your time. Do you take all your sick time, vacation days, and personal days?

The closer to perfection you want your work to be, the more time it will take. Is there a point at which you can say that the extra time needed to make something better simply isn't worth it? Remember that perfection is the enemy of the good. To get something exactly right may well mean the neglect of other important things, such as your family.

Perhaps it is possible to bring your child with you to work. Younger children will need daycare. If your company doesn't have a daycare center, can you petition for one? There may be other parents in the same position as you, and together you can convince the company to create one or find one nearby that you can use. The convincing evidence on daycare studies is that children in daycare don't suffer any setbacks, as long as the quality of the care is good and parents remain involved in their children's lives.

If your child is older, she may be able to spend some of the time with you at work during school holidays. Introduce her to your co-workers, let her know the place where you spend most of your time.

Consider the trade-offs you make between money and time. A higher-paying job may mean a longer commuting time. Think about what the extra money will bring you, but also consider what the additional time at home may mean.

Take time during the day to stay in contact with your children. Call them regularly, send them faxes and e-mails. Your employer may offer flextime so you can work when your children are at school and be home when they are. If you can afford it, see if it is possible to job share so that you can work part-time.

Before taking work home at night or on the weekend ask yourself whether it is really necessary. Maybe someone else could do the job just as well. You may not get the promotion you wanted as quickly as you want, but you may end up with a better relationship with your child in return.

Computers, faxes, cell phones, and beepers make it increasingly possible for you to work from home (although it isn't much of an option for blue-collar workers). But working from home also has its downside. Home used to be a respite from work, a quiet place for family, at least for the major bread-winner. But if work and home are identical, then there is no getting away, then you may begin to feel like the housewife of the fifties who couldn't wait to get out of the house once the children were grown. Instead of working eight hours a day, the home worker is constantly working, the family is being constantly interrupted. There are things you can do to protect your time with your children, such as giving them your full attention when you are with them. Set aside time that is just for your children, don't answer the phone, ignore the fax, and forget about e-mail. That time belongs to your children, not your employer. Remember that working at home is meant to give you more time with your family, not make you a slave to the job.

Finally, make a list of values relative to work and family. Why you work, what you want from a job, how much money is enough, what you are willing to do for more money, what you are willing to give up to get it, and how do your children fit into the scheme of things?

40.

Take an Interest in the World Outside Your Home

You already have your hands full, so this step may sound like extra work to you. But I'm not suggesting you take on something you don't want to do or aren't ready to try. However, there are things you can do to bring the concerns of the larger world into your own home. The possibilities are many and the involvement ranges from the more passive, such as writing a check, to the more active, such as being a literacy volunteer or having an exchange student live with your family. Remember, your children will take their cues from you. If you care about people, so will they.

Your efforts don't have to be large. No one person is expected to save the world, but each of us can have a small part in making the world a better place. The French have a saying: Small rivers make great lakes.

You will teach your children about being a responsible person by writing a check to your favorite charity or volunteering for a walk-a-thon to raise money for a good cause. You can teach a valuable lesson by bringing food to a sick neighbor or driving an elderly neighbor to the doctor or donating cast-off clothes to those in need.

You may want to take holiday time as an occasion to contribute to a charity or volunteer at an agency. Many families help the needy at Christmastime. You may want to adopt a child who is less fortunate than you. In times of disasters, newspapers provide addresses of organizations accepting donations of money and goods.

It is easier than ever to find outlets for your generous impulses by going online. You want to do a good deed but not go far from home? "Impact Online" (www.impactonline.org) is a volunteer-matching database. Type in your ZIP code, and you will find all sorts of opportunities. Within five miles of my own home on Long Island I found five opportunities ranging from peer counseling at the Mental Health Association of Nassau County to meeting foreign students through a local university. You can also show your concern for the world by being a socially responsible shopper. If you buy something from "give" (www.igive.com), 15 percent of the purchase price is donated to your cause; furthermore each visit to the site without a purchase can earn your association up to four cents.

For the internationally minded there is "The Hunger Site" (www.thehungersite.com) where company sponsors pay a half cent for each click to help feed the hungry through the United Nations. You can use this site once a day, and each time you'll donate one and a quarter cups of rice, wheat, corn, or other staple food to a hungry person.

Afterword

Many people think that morality and happiness are always at odds with one another. Once I had lunch with a well-known poet who wore colorful ties and liked to sing as part of his readings. When he asked me about myself, I told him that I was the leader of an organization concerned with ethics in everyday living, he dismissed me out-of-hand.

He didn't want anyone dictating to him how he should live. This was especially ironic, because he had been a leading voice in protests against the war in Vietnam.

The problem was he confused being ethical with being moralistic. And moralistic people are scolds, they wag their fingers at others, they tell other people what to do, and they are grim faced. The image that comes to mind is that of the strict Puritans condemning every act of pleasure.

Of course, what the poet was complaining about wasn't ethical behavior but narrow-minded self-righteousness.

He was also wrong in thinking that morality and happiness can't come together. Actually, when psychologists Ann Colby and William Damon looked closely at twenty-three people who had made significant contributions to the betterment of their communities, they found three common characteristics. First, the moral exemplars had "exceptional clarity about what they believe is right and about their own personal responsibility to act on those beliefs." Second, their moral goals "in large part constituted their very identities." And third, they had a positive approach to life, enjoyed their work, and were optimistic. Almost without exception, they were extremely happy and fulfilled.

Wouldn't the world be a better place if we raised children who were both moral and happy? It is possible to do. I hope that this book has provided you with a way in which you can be the parent of the child whom others can point to with pride, not because of what he has achieved but because of the kind of person he has become.

Selected References

Introduction

Rest, James R., *Moral Development: Advances in Research and Theory*, New York: Praeger, 1986.

Feelings

Bayley, John, "Elegy for Iris," *The New Yorker*, July 27, 1998.

Damasio, Antonio R., *Descartes' Error: Emotion, Reason and the Human Brain*, New York: G. P. Putnam's Sons, 1994.

De Waal, Frans, *Good Natured: The Origins of Right and Wrong in Humans and Other Animals*, Cambridge: Harvard University Press, 1996.

Gaylin, Willard, *Feelings: Our Vital Signs*, New York: Ballatine Books, 1979.

Hoffman, Martin, "Is Altruism Part of Human Nature?" *Journal of Personality and Social Psychology*, 40, 1981.

Levinas, Emanuel, *Entre Nosotros*, Valencia: Pretextos, 1933.

Oliner, Samuel, P. Oliner, *The Altruistic Personality: Rescuers of Jews in Nazi Germany*, New York: The Press, 1988.

Sherman, Nancy, "The Place of Emotions in Kantian Morality," in *Identity, Character and Morality: Essays in Moral Psychology*, Owen Flanagan and A. O. Rorty, Cambridge: The MIT Press, 1990.

Wilson, E. O., *Sociobiology: The New Synthesis*, Cambridge: Harvard University Press, 1975.

Reason

Aristotle, *Nichomachean Ethics: Book Two*, (trans. Martin Gotwald), New York: Macmillan, 1962.

Dobrin, Arthur, *Love Your Neighbor: Stories of Values and Virtues*, New York: Scholastic, 1999.

Grusec, J., J. J. Goodnow, "Impact of Parental Discipline on the Child's Internalization of Values: A Reconceptualization of Current Points of View," *Developmental Psychology*, 20, 1994.

Kegan, Robert, *The Evolving Self: Problems and Process in Human Development*, Cambridge: Harvard University Press, 1982.

Kohlberg, Lawrence, *The Philosophy of Moral Development: Essays on Moral Development, Vol 1*, New York: Harper & Row, 1984.

Piaget, Jean, *Moral Judgment of the Child*, New York: The Free Press, 1965.

Rest, James R., *Moral Development: Advances in Research and Theory*, New York: Praeger, 1986.

Sprinthall, N., J. Scott, "Promoting Psychological Development, Math Achievement and Success Attribution of Female Students Through Deliberate Psychological Education," *Journal of Counseling Psychology*, 36, 1989.

Self-Esteem

Abdallah, Taisir M., "Self-esteem and Locus of Control of College Men in Saudi Arabia," *Psychological Reports*, 65, 1989.

Berman, Philip L. (ed.), *The Courage of Conviction*, New York: Ballantine Books, 1986.

Gibran, Kahil, *The Prophet*, New York: Alfred A. Knopf, 1961.

Hacohen, Shmuel Avidor, *Touching Heaven Touching Earth: Hassidic Humor & Wit*, Tel-Aviv: Sadan Publishing, 1976.

Leeson, Nick with Edward Whitley, *Rogue Trader: How I Brought Down Barings Banks and Shook the Financial World*, Boston: Little, Brown & Co., 1996.

Martin, Mike W., *Everyday Morality: An Introduction to Applied Ethics*, Belmont, CA: Wadswoth Publishing Co., 1989.

Midlarsky, Elizabeth, "Helping In Late Life," in *Embracing the Other: Philosophical, Psychological, and Historical Perspectives on Altruism*, Pearl Oliner, S. P. Oliner, L. Baron, L. A. Blum, D. K. Krebs, M. Z. Smolenska (eds.), New York: New York University Press, 1992.

Mruk, Chris, *Self-esteem: Research, Theory, and Practice*, New York: Springer Publishing Co., 1995.

Newsday, February 8, 1995.

Tashakor, Abbas, V. Thompson, "Race Differences in Self-perception and Locus of Control During Adolescence and Early Adulthood: Methodological Implications," *Genetic, Social, and General Psychology Monographs*, 117, 1991.

Wynne, Edward A., K. Ryan, *Reclaiming Our Schools: A Handbook on Teaching Character, Academics, and Discipline*, New York: Macmillan, 1993.

Discipline

Fogelman, Eva, *Conscience and Courage: Rescuers of Jews During the Holocaust*, New York: Anchor Books, 1994.

Freud, Sigmund, *Civilization and Its Discontents*, New York: W. W. Norton, 1962.

Frijda, Nico, B. Mesquita, "The Social Roles and Functions of Emotions," in *Emotion and Culture: Empirical Studies of Mutual Influence*, Shinobu Kitayama and H. R. Markus (eds.), Washington, D.C.: American Psychological Association, 1994.

Lewis, Helen Block, *Shame and Guilt in Neurosis*, New York: International Universities Press, 1971.

Morris, Herbert, "The Decline of Guilt," *Ethics*, Vol. 99, October 1988.

Schneider, Carl, *Shame, Exposure, and Privacy*, Boston: Beacon Press, 1977.

Steinberg, Laurence, *Beyond the Classroom: Why School Reform Has Failed and What Parents Need to Know*, New York: Simon & Schuster, 1996.

Habits

Damon, William, *Greater Expectations: Overcoming the Culture of Indulgence In America's Homes and Schools*, New York: The Free Press, 1995.

Hallie, Philip, *Lest Innocent Blood Be Shed: The Story of the Village of Le Chambon and How Goodness Happened There*, New York: Harperperennial Library, 1994.

James, William, *Writings: 1878–1899*, New York: Library Classics of the United States, 1992.

MacIntyre, Alasdair, *After Virtue: A Study In Moral Theory*, Notre Dame, IN: University of Notre Dame Press, 1981.

Maimonide: His Wisdom for Our Times, Gilbert Rosenthal, translator and editor, New York: Funk and Wagnalls, 1969.

Rosenthal, Robert, *Pygmalian in the Classroom: Teacher Expectation and Pupils' Intellectual Development*, New York: Holt, Rinehard & Winston, 1968.

Sauvage, Pierre, "Weapons of the Spirit," New York: First Run Features/Icarus Films, 1988.

Staub, Ervin, "The Roots of Prosocial and Antisocial Behavior in Persons and Groups: Environmental Influence, Personality, Culture, and Socialization," in *Moral Development: An Introduction*, William Kurtines and J. L. Gewirtz (eds.), Needham Heights, MA: Allyn & Bacon, 1995.

Wuthnow, Robert, *Acts of Compassion: Caring for Others and Helping Ourselves*, Princeton: Princeton University Press, 1991.

Prejudice

Aronson, Elliot, *The Social Animal*, New York: W. H. Freeman, 1992.

Dewey, John, *Types of Thinking Including a Survey of Greek Philosophy*, New York: Philosophical Library, 1984.

Kaplan, Abraham, *In Pursuit of Wisdom*, New York: Glance Publishing Co., 1977.

Rodgers, Richard, O. Hammerstein, "You Have to be Taught," from *South Pacific*, 1949.

Shakespeare, William, *The Merchant of Venice*, in *The Complete Works of Shakespeare*, Hardin Craig, ed. Chicago: Scott, Foresman and Company, 1961.

Staub, Ervin, "The Origins of Caring, Helping, and Non-aggression," in *Embracing the Other: Philosophical, Psychological, and Historical Perspectives on Altruism*, Pearl M. Oliner, S. P. Oliner,

L. Baron, L. A. Blum, D. K. Koreas, M. Z. Smolenska (eds.), New York: New York University Press, 1992.

Values

Colby, Ann, W. Damon, "The Development of Extraordinary Moral Commitment," in *Morality in Everyday Life: Developmental Perspectives*, Cambridge: Cambridge University Press, 1995.

Damon, William, *The Moral Child: Nurturing Children's Moral Growth*, New York: The Free Press, 1988.

Dosick, Wayne, *Golden Rules: The Ten Ethical Values Parents Need To Teach Their Children*, San Francisco: Harper, 1995.

Erikson, Erik, *Identity and the Life Cycle*, New York: W. W. Norton, 1994.

Kekes, John, *Facing Evil*, Princeton: Princeton University Press, 1990.

Shweder, Richard, A. M. Mahapatra, and J. A. Miller, "Culture and Moral Development," in *The Emergence of Morality in Young Children*, Jerome Kagan and S. Lamb (eds.), Chicago: University of Chicago Press, 1987.

White, Stephen, J. E. O'Brien, "What Is a Hero? An Exploratory Study of Students' Conceptions of Heroes," *Journal of Moral Education*, Vol. 28, 1999.

Community

American Academy of Pediatrics, "Media Violence," *Pediatrics*, 95, 1995.

Araton, Harvey, "A Misguided and Warped Value System," *N.Y. Times*, June 28, 1997.

Blankenhorn, David, "The Possibility of Civil Society," in *Seeds of Virtue: Sources of Competence, Character and Citizenship in American Society*, Mary Ann Glendon, D. Blankenhorn (eds.), Lanham, MD: Madison Books, 1995.

Hacker, Andrew, *Two Nations: Black and White, Separate, Hostile, Unequal*, New York: Scribners, 1992.

Johnson, Byron, D. Larson, T. Pitts, "Religious Programs, Institutional Adjustment, and Recidivism Among Former Inmates in Prison Fellowship Programs," *Justice Quarterly*, 14, 1997.

Kubey, Robert, M. Csikszentmihalyi, *Television and the Quality of Life: How Viewing Shapes Everyday Experience*, Hillsdale, NJ: Lawrence Erlbaum Associates, Publishers, 1990.

Nucci, Larry, "Challenging Conventional Wisdom About Morality: The Domain Approach to Values Education," in *Moral Development and Character Education*, Larry P. Nucci (ed.), Berkley: McCutchan Publishing Corporation, 1989.

Pipher, Mary, *The Shelter of Each Other: Rebuilding Our Families*, New York: Grosset/Putnam, 1996.

Index